Sue Carter Collins, PhD

The Mind Mastery Architect™

From Mastering Your Mind to Mastering Your Life

A Woman's Guide to Purpose and Self-Empowerment

Foreword by Lisa Nichols, Bestselling
Author & Motivational Speaker

Sue Carter Collins, PhD

The Mind Mastery Architect™

From Mastering Your Mind to Mastering Your Life

A Woman's Guide to Purpose and Self-Empowerment

Published by Dr. Sue Carter Collins in collaboration
with Bold Publishing
USA

Copyright Page

From Mastering Your Mind to Mastering Your Life: A Woman's Guide to Purpose and Self-Empowerment
© 2025 by Sue Carter Collins. All rights reserved.

Library of Congress Control Number (LCCN): 2025922682

ISBN (paperback): 979-8-9940534-0-9
Printed in the United States of America
Publisher & inquiries: Bold Publishing • New York
Author contact: https://www.linkedin.com/in/drsuecartercollins/

Interior design: Sophie Hanks

Master your mind, and you reclaim your life.
The battlefield is within, not without.
Victory comes not through force,
but through awareness, alignment, and self-discipline.

~ Dr. Sue Carter Collins

Dedication

To my beloved mother, Vera Bell Carter—my first teacher, my fiercest protector, and the embodiment of grace under fire.
Your prayers built the foundation upon which this work stands.
Your unwavering love shaped my soul, and your wisdom continues to echo in every word I write and speak.
This book is part of your legacy.

For every woman who has ever felt like an outsider in the rooms she worked so hard to enter.
For every high achiever who doubted her worth, despite the degrees, the titles, and the accolades.
For every brilliant mind silenced by fear, perfectionism, or the invisible weight of impostor syndrome—
This book is for you.

You were never unqualified.
You were never too much.
You were never not enough.
You were powerful all along.
Now it's time to remember.

CONTENTS

Foreword by Lisa Nichols

There are moments when a book isn't just written — it's *birthed.* Born out of fire. Out of surrender. Out of the kind of truth that doesn't just shift your mindset — it rearranges your soul.

When I first met **Dr. Sue Carter Collins**, I recognized that kind of truth in her. Not in her credentials or her confidence — but in her *becoming.* Behind the titles and degrees was a heart that was cracking open, a soul quietly whispering, *I'm ready to finish healing so I can help others heal too.*

We met at my **Dynamic Women's Retreat in the Bahamas**, surrounded by powerhouse women from all over the world — women with big dreams, big fears, and even bigger callings. The room pulsed with purpose. Dr. Sue had all the right credentials — a J.D., a Ph.D., decades of accomplishment — but what she didn't yet know was that her divine assignment didn't require credentials. It required presence. It required surrender. It required *her.*

She told me later she almost didn't come. Fear had crept in. That familiar voice whispered, *Will I belong? Am I enough?* And like every courageous woman who chooses purpose over perfection, she showed up anyway.

I'll never forget one particular exercise — a blindfolded trust walk. It wasn't just about following another's lead; it was about releasing control. As Dr. Sue stood there trembling, tears welling, I watched her take a breath... and then she let go. She stepped forward, blindfolded, guided only by faith. That moment was her beginning — a step from knowing into becoming.

That's who Dr. Sue is. She doesn't teach from theory; she teaches from *truth.* She doesn't talk about transformation; she *is* transformation. Her journey — from academia and societal expectation to radical self-love and divine alignment — is the very embodiment of the work she now brings to the world.

When I later read *From Mastering Your Mind to Mastering Your Life,* I felt the same vibration I saw in her that day — the sound of a woman who answered her calling. This book is her sacred yes to the whisper she once heard: *"My people are hungry. Feed my sheep."*

Whew. When I read that line, I had to close the book and breathe. Because that's what purpose sounds like. It's not glamorous. It's not easy. It's not about ego. It's about obedience — the kind that costs you comfort but restores your soul.

In these pages, Dr. Sue hands us the keys to our own freedom. She names the pain — the mental cages we build, the masks we wear, the stories that keep us small — and then she shows us the way out. Her **Self-Empowerment Breakthrough Process**™ is not theory; it's *testimony turned into technology.* It's wisdom wrapped in practicality, spirituality grounded in neuroscience.

She teaches that mastery of the mind isn't about control; it's about *consciousness.* It's learning to see the stories you've been living, to rewrite them with compassion, and to live from the truth of who you really are. She brings together science, spirit, and lived experience in a way that feels both deeply human and divinely guided.

I've always said: transformation doesn't happen because you *want* it. It happens because you're *willing.*
Willing to tell yourself the truth.
Willing to peel back the layers.
Willing to meet your reflection with compassion instead of criticism.

Dr. Sue stands as your mirror, mentor, and midwife through that process. She shows you how to release the lies of not-enoughness and remember what God already declared: *You are worthy. You are powerful. You are divine.*

This is not a book to *read*; it's a book to *practice.* Each chapter is a permission slip to pause, breathe, and reclaim the pieces of yourself you've left behind. Every page is an altar of awareness — a place to lay down old stories and pick up your peace.

As you move through her five-phase journey — reflection, reimagining, release, reprogramming, and recreation — you'll recognize yourself again. You'll remember that freedom doesn't come from doing more; it comes from *being* more of who you already are.

So don't just turn the pages — *work* them. Let them work you. Let them stretch you. Let them love you back to your wholeness.

Because the version of you waiting on the other side of this book? She's powerful. She's peaceful. She's free.

And she's already inside you.

With love, light, and unwavering belief in your becoming,

Lisa Nichols
Motivational Speaker | Author | CEO, Motivating the Masses

Preface

"When I dare to be powerful—
to use my strength in the service of my vision—
then it becomes less and less important
whether I am afraid."

~ Audre Lorde

Feed My Sheep

On the outside, I had it all.

I was a tenured Associate Professor with a secure income and impeccable professional credentials. I lived in a beautiful house. I wore designer clothes. I had money in the bank and two cars in the garage—one of them a Jaguar. By every external measure, I had arrived.

But inside, I was falling apart.

I carried more than the weight of my own ambition. I carried the weight of my race and gender, the burden of representation, and the invisible pressure to be twice as good for half the recognition. Like many high-achieving Black women, I internalized the message that my worth had to be proven—over and over again.

So I chased degrees like they were oxygen. I have five advanced degrees—BS, MS, JD, PhD, and BMsc—not because I was collecting accolades, but because I was trying to silence a voice within that whispered: *You're still not enough.* But no matter how many diplomas I hung on the wall, that voice never stopped.

What I now understand is that I was suffering from a deeply rooted, socially reinforced dis-ease: *not-enoughism.* It was born from racism. From sexism. From systems that told me who I could not be. And from generations of struggle encoded into my body before I even had a name for it.

Although I had the outer life of success, inside I felt like an imposter.

The Breaking Point

Death comes slowly to some of us. It comes in the form of life breaking apart—of losing the things we hold most dear. My love life was in shambles. I was facing financial ruin. And alcohol had become my go-to solution to make it through the night. Despite all I had accomplished, I felt deeply alone—surrounded by people but seen by no one. I was empty, disconnected from joy, questioning my purpose, and spiritually exhausted.

But no one knew. I hid my pain well.

I wore the mask of success like a second skin: I laughed in meetings, supported clients, and encouraged students. I performed excellence. But inside, I could feel the life force draining out of me.

I'll never forget Tuesday, July 17, 2012. That was the day I seriously considered ending my life. It started out as just a normal day. I worked. I went home. I drank. It had become an endless cycle, and I was spiraling—going nowhere fast.

The life I had built, brick by brick, was crumbling before my eyes. Fear and depression were my constant companions. I realized I had lost myself—and I was terrified of losing everything else.

In the darkness of that night, I knew I had to make a choice: either continue down the path of self-destruction or make a new start.

The next day, I walked into Alcoholics Anonymous. That was my Hail Mary. I didn't have a Plan B. If AA didn't work, I didn't know what I would do—or where I would be. It was my last hope to save a life that looked perfect from the outside but felt like a prison within.

July 18, 2012. That was the day I met the God of my being—not in church, not in ritual, but in the rooms of AA, where I learned that alcohol addiction is the great equalizer. In that space of surrender and radical honesty—surrounded by people from all walks of life— my healing journey began in earnest.

The Long Road to Return

As this book goes to press, it has been 13 years since my last drink. The healing that followed wasn't instant—and it wasn't easy.

Between 2012 and 2018, I entered the deepest transformation period of my life… and the most difficult. In addition to undergoing therapy, I studied metaphysics, neuroscience, trauma recovery, and spiritual psychology. I dove headfirst into personal development—not just to teach it, but to embody it. I confronted my patterns, identified my triggers, acknowledged my pain, and embraced the shadow self I had hidden so well behind my degrees and accomplishments.

In 2018, I published *Return to Self: 5 Keys to Emotional & Spiritual Freedom*—the first testimony of my transformation. In it, I shared a five-step process—the Return to Self Transformation Process—that I used to facilitate my own healing. Since then, I've refined and renamed it the Self-Empowerment Breakthrough Method™ (the SEB Method™). I've used it to successfully coach hundreds of high-achieving women.

The Call That Changed Everything

I didn't plan to write this book. In fact, I wasn't sure I was up to the task. I had retired from the university. I was no longer drinking. I had started a new life in a new state. And though I was still adjusting, I felt happy. The thought of writing another book was almost overwhelming. Was I ready to commit to all that it would entail?

But here's what I've discovered: often, man's plan is not God's plan.

So it was with me and this book.

In mid-March of this year, while sitting in a small country church one Sunday morning, I got the call—not on the phone, not from a platform or a podium, but from the still, small voice within:

"My people are hungry. Feed my sheep."

I sat there frozen in time. With my eyes closed I beheld the vision. As far as my spiritual eyes could see, I saw human figures with their heads tilted back and their mouths open. The words leaving my mouth were going directly into theirs.

And once again, I heard: *"My people are hungry. Feed my sheep."*

I knew, without question, I was being given a divine assignment—not just to coach, but to speak and teach. To reveal to others the knowledge I had gained through my studies and lived experiences. To serve humanity by guiding others into the kind of inner peace and freedom I had achieved.

This book is born from that call.

It carries within it the weight of my breaking, the energy of my surrender, the clarity of my purpose, and the power of the framework that helped me heal.

The Wisdom I Asked For

Before God calls you, He will always prepare you.

After successfully completing my first year in AA, I began to pursue a career as a Life Coach. In addition to learning how to coach and support others, I embraced the spiritual path of personal development. I learned to meditate and listen for divine guidance.

One day, while sitting quietly, I heard the voice I had come to recognize as God say:
"What would you ask of Me?"

I didn't respond immediately. And when I did, I didn't ask for fame or fortune. Recalling one of my favorite stories from the Bible, I said:

"Give me the wisdom of Solomon and make me the embodiment of peace. That wherever I go and whomever I touch, I may leave them in a more peaceful place than I found them."

It bears noting that when you ask for wisdom and peace, you will be given experiences in life that require you to grow into them.

So getting there wasn't immediate. And it wasn't easy. It was a process.

But one day, I realized I was no longer the person I used to be. I had been stripped of my old self—the one I had clung to during life's struggles, the one I had embraced in order to survive, the one I had grown used to, even in her suffering. I was rebuilt. Rewired.

Now, I seek to teach others what I've learned from my experiences— to share what I know—not perfectly, but transparently and authentically.

Why I Wrote This Book

This is not a book of easy answers.
It is not for the faint of heart, or for those looking to bypass the real work of healing.

It is a map, a method, and a mirror.

It is for high-achieving women who are tired of performing and are ready to embody wholeness. It is for those who feel the ache beneath their success and know, deep down, there must be more. It is for those who are tired of living in struggle, who are ready to go beyond survival to thrival.

If that's you—this book is your invitation.

You don't have to burn your life down to transform.
You don't have to abandon your brilliance to find your soul.
You just have to be willing to turn inward—with honesty, with compassion, and with vision.

So today I offer this work as a woman who wore the mask of success and almost didn't make it.
As a woman who was brought to her knees and rose again with a vow to live differently.
To lead differently.
To rewire her mind.
To live in alignment with the divine.
To embody a new story.

"Feed my sheep," He said.
And so I shall.

From my mouth to yours—this is my offering.

"When the old self dissolves, the divine design emerges. From the ashes of despair, a new story rises—one of wholeness, freedom, and light. In surrender, the soul remembers its power."
~Dr. Sue Carter Collins

Introduction

"The privilege of a lifetime is to become who you truly are."

~ C.G. Jung

This Is Where the Real Work Begins

You did everything you were supposed to do.
Earned the degrees. Built the résumé. Played by the rules.

From the outside, it looks like you made it.
But on the inside… something is missing.

You wake up wondering: *Is this really all there is?*
Your mind won't stop spinning—looping the same anxious thoughts, replaying old conversations, second-guessing your every move.

You can feel it in your gut.
You're holding your breath, trying hard to maintain a version of yourself you no longer recognize.

Consider this your wake-up call.

Hear me when I say: you're not falling apart.
You're experiencing a rebirth.

What This Book Is (and What It's Not)

This is not a book about surface-level mindset.
It's not about toxic positivity, motivational fluff, or bypassing pain with spiritual language.

This book is a return to the root.

It is a guide for those who have reached the summit of achievement—and for those enmeshed in the climb—only to realize they left themselves behind.

This is for the woman who is outwardly successful but inwardly unsettled.
Who has "done the work" and still feels stuck.
Who can pour into everyone else—but doesn't yet know how to pour into herself.

This book is your invitation to come home—not to the version of you shaped by expectation, but to the version of you born whole and encoded with divine wisdom.

Why Mind Mastery Is the Place to Begin

Transformation doesn't begin with strategy.
It begins with awareness.

Your life is a reflection of the thoughts, beliefs, and energetic imprints you carry—many of which were formed before you could even speak. Most of us live not from who we truly are, but from what we were taught to believe about who we are.

Science tells us that much of this programming happens early in life, when the subconscious is wide open and impressionable. The patterns formed in those years quietly direct as much as 90–95% of your behavior. Spiritual wisdom has echoed this truth for centuries, teaching that "all is mind"—that the outer world mirrors the vibration of your dominant thoughts, emotions, and expectations.

The message is simple: you cannot change your life without changing your relationship to your mind.

This doesn't mean silencing your thoughts or waging war with your brain. It means learning to see, decode, and gently recode the patterns that have shaped your reality—approaching them with awareness, compassion, and divine guidance.

That is the work of mind mastery.

What Makes This Different

The Mind Mastery Solution™ introduced in this book is not a generic mindset formula.
It is a multidimensional framework that draws from:

- Neuroscience and cognitive psychology
- Metaphysical laws and spiritual principles
- Energy awareness and emotional integration
- Trauma-informed healing practices
- Years of lived experience, study, and spiritual surrender

At the heart of the Mind Mastery Solution is a transformational method I call the Self-Empowerment Breakthrough Process™—a five-phase journey that helps you:

1. **Reflect** – Become aware of the subconscious patterns and stories shaping your life
2. **Reimagine** – Create a vision of your empowered self
3. **Release** – Let go of what no longer serves your becoming
4. **Reprogram** – Install new beliefs, thought patterns, and energetic codes
5. **Recreate** – Embody your truth and live your reimagined life with coherence and courage

You'll learn about this process in depth later in the book.

For now, understand this: transformation is not about becoming someone new.
It is about returning to who you were before the world told you who you had to be.

What You Can Expect

This book is divided into three parts:

Part I. Cracking the Code: Understanding the Mind in Action
This part is foundational. Understanding how the brain, belief systems, emotional set points, and social conditioning shape your inner world is a necessary prerequisite to mastering your mind and transforming your life.

Part II. The Self-Empowerment Breakthrough Process™
This is a step-by-step walkthrough of the five phases of transformation—integrating knowledge from spiritual, psychological, neuroscience, and energy perspectives—to help you shift your inner programming and embody your empowered self.

Part III. Mind Mastery in Action

The final section teaches you how to live your reimagined life in real time—led by intuition, anchored in purpose, and unapologetically whole.

Throughout the book, you'll find human stories, reflection questions, and tools to help you deepen your awareness and sustain your transformation.

This is more than a book to read—it's a guide to practice. Each chapter will invite you to pause, reflect, and apply the principles directly to your life. By the end, you won't just understand the power of mind mastery—you'll be living it, with tools you can return to again and again.

My Promise to You

This is not a book you skim.
It's a book you work through. Breathe through. Live through.

It will challenge you, disarm you, and invite you to meet yourself with new eyes.

I will not walk ahead of you.
I'll walk beside you—shoulder to shoulder, heart to heart—with tools I've tested in the fire of my own transformation and those of my clients.

I'm not here to fix you.
You're not broken.

I'm here to help you remember your power, reclaim your mind, and rise into the life you were designed to live.

If you're ready to embrace your greatness and lay hold of the life your soul remembers—turn the page.

---

*"Once you awaken, you cannot go back to sleep.
You were made for more—and now you know it."*
~ Dr. Sue Carter Collins

Reader's Guide

How to Engage With This Book

"Transformation begins not in reading, but in how you engage."

~Dr. Sue Carter Collins

This book is not meant to be skimmed. It is a guide, a map, and a mirror. Its power lies not just in the words on the page, but in the way you choose to interact with them. To experience the fullness of what mind mastery can offer, I encourage you to read actively, reflect honestly, and apply consistently.

Here's how to get the most out of this book:

1. Read Slowly and Intentionally

Take your time with each chapter. Allow the concepts, stories, and practices to settle into your awareness. This is not about speed; it's about depth.

2. Pause and Reflect

Throughout the chapters, you'll find *Pause & Reflect* prompts. These are gentle invitations to stop, breathe, and check in with your own experience. Use them as moments of self-inquiry and integration.

3. Engage with the Deep Dive Questions

At the end of each chapter, you'll find *Deep Dive Questions.* These are designed to help you examine your own patterns, beliefs, and stories more deeply. Write your answers down. Speak them aloud. Share them in safe spaces. The more you engage, the more transformation you'll experience.

4. Notice Your Resistance

Some questions may stir discomfort. That's not failure—it's growth. Resistance is a sign you're brushing up against the edges of your old programming. Rather than avoiding it, lean in with compassion.

5. Practice, Don't Just Think

Mind mastery isn't achieved by information alone. It requires practice. Use the tools and exercises you encounter as living experiments. Try them out. Observe how your mind and body respond. Repeat them until new neural and energetic patterns begin to form.

6. Bring Your Whole Self

This book invites you to bring not only your intellect, but also your heart, your spirit, and your body. Transformation happens when all levels of your being—mental, emotional, physical, and spiritual—are engaged in the process.

A Final Word Before You Begin

You don't need to be perfect, ready, or fearless to start this journey. You only need to be willing. If you show up with openness and honesty, this book will meet you exactly where you are—and guide you to where you're meant to go.

PART I

Cracking the Code – Understanding the Mind

Every transformation begins with awareness. In this opening part, you'll learn to observe the mind as both architect and storyteller—to see how thoughts, emotions, and beliefs interact to shape your lived experience. As you begin decoding the patterns of your conditioning, you'll uncover the invisible programs that drive behavior and perception.

This is where the journey of mind mastery begins: with curiosity, honesty, and a willingness to see yourself clearly. Awareness is not the end of transformation—it is the invitation to it.

Chapter 1

Unlocking the Mental Cage

"The most common way people give up their power is by thinking they don't have any."

~ Alice Walker

Success Isn't the Same as Freedom

It starts quietly.

Every day, somewhere, a woman wakes up before dawn. The alarm doesn't startle her—she's already been lying there, mind racing. She runs through her checklist for the day ahead: meetings to lead, emails to send, a team to manage, a family to tend to. She rises, dresses with precision, and wears her competence like armor.

At work, she is efficient. Articulate. Respected. Her inbox is overflowing because everyone wants her input. Her schedule is tight because everyone values her presence.

She moves through the day like a woman who has it all together. And yet...

When she gets home, silence greets her louder than applause ever did. She pours a glass of wine to relax—she doesn't call it coping. She scrolls. She eats without tasting. She tells herself she should be grateful; she has a successful career.

But underneath the gratitude is a whisper: *Is this it? Is this all there is?*
She knows something is missing. But what it is... she's just not sure.

Her heart aches.
She's successful.
But what she wants seems to elude her.
What she wants is inner peace, joy, and freedom.

Pause & Reflect: *When have I looked successful on the outside but felt disconnected on the inside?*

The Myth of Arrival

So many high-achieving women live this way.

We're raised on the promise that success is the end game. That if we earn the degrees, secure the titles, build the career, and look the part, we'll finally feel whole—we'll have it made.

For some of us, that belief was survival. As Black women, and women of color, the burden of representation meant we didn't just decide to strive for excellence—we had to. We worked twice as hard to prove our worth, navigating both systemic bias and inherited trauma with a smile on our faces and perfection in our step.

And yet, despite all we accomplish, a silent ache persists.

The truth is: success was never designed to liberate us. It was designed to validate us within the system that caged us.

We followed the map they gave us. We reached the final destination, but the location is foreign. The victory feels hollow.

Pause & Reflect: *What was I promised about success, and has it truly delivered what I hoped it would?*

Naming the Cage

What do you call it when everything looks good on paper, but your soul knows you're living a lie?

I call it the mental cage.

It is not a failure of success. It is the unquestioned programming behind it.

The mental cage is built from beliefs we didn't choose:

- *I have to prove myself to be worthy.*
- *If I stop to rest, I'll fall behind.*
- *Being strong means never needing help.*

- *If I'm not achieving, I won't be valued.*
- *I need one more degree (or certification) to be good enough.*

These beliefs become walls in a mental prison. Invisible to all but reinforced by repetition, performance, and reward. Many times, we don't even realize we're trapped—until we've outgrown the version of ourselves we built to survive.

Pause & Reflect: *Which beliefs in my life feel like survival rules rather than personal truth?*

The Illusion of Success

The mental cage. I know this space well.

For years, I lived in it.

I had five advanced degrees, a tenured position as an Associate Professor, a home in a well-to-do neighborhood, and a professional reputation others admired. I was the woman others came to for wisdom, laughter, and guidance.

And yet, I carried within me a pain I couldn't share—and didn't know how to name.

I struggled with impostor syndrome long before I had the language for it. I often felt like I didn't belong in the rooms I occupied—even when I was leading them. My credentials said I was qualified; my friends and colleagues said I was intelligent, but I could never fully silence the voice within that whispered a litany of songs: *You don't really belong here. You don't know enough. You're not very smart. You've got to prove your worth.*

I felt profoundly alone. Not physically—I was always surrounded by people: students, faculty, friends, clients, community. But emotionally, I felt unseen.

I wore the mask of happiness and invisibility simultaneously—laughing, listening, giving, and guiding while concealing my own emotional pain.

It was as if the more I succeeded, the more I lost myself, and the more invisible I became.

Pause & Reflect: *When have I worn the mask of success while silently carrying pain?*

The Cost of Containment

Living in the mental cage has a cost; a quiet, cumulative cost.

It looks like over-functioning. Over-giving. Over-analyzing.
It looks like perfectionism, people-pleasing, anxiety, emotional detachment, and burnout.
It feels like chronic tension in the body—an ache in your heart that can't be defined. A knot in your gut that won't go away. Bouts of depression that drugs can't cure and friends and family don't understand.

It sounds like looping thoughts that just won't stop. Like rumination, day after day.

We learn to survive by shrinking the parts of us that feel too much, want too much, or question too much.

We downplay our spiritual needs. We minimize our emotional truth.
We intellectualize our pain.
We smile on the outside while silencing our truth within.

We are high-functioning, high-performing women…
And we are slowly breaking.

Pause & Reflect: *Which costs of the mental cage do I recognize in my own life?*

What Science and Spirit Says About Our Quality of Life

Neuroscience tells us the brain is, above all else, a prediction machine. Its job is survival, not happiness. It prefers the familiar—even when the familiar is painful—because predictability feels safer than uncertainty.

That's why old thought patterns, even destructive ones, are so hard to break. To the brain, the familiar equals survival. To step outside those patterns feels threatening, even when, consciously, we know it could set us free.

Psychologist John Bargh's research in the 1990s revealed that much of our daily behavior is guided by subconscious programming and cognitive bias. Biologist Bruce Lipton later expanded on this, demonstrating that as much as ninety to ninety-five percent of our behavior is influenced by patterns laid down before we were even fully aware of ourselves. These programs include trauma responses, inherited survival strategies, and the subtle lessons of our upbringing.

Until we bring those subconscious loops into awareness, they quietly run the show.

Metaphysically, this is explained by the Law of Correspondence: *As within, so without.* Our outer lives reflect our inner narratives. If the story we carry is one of unworthiness, scarcity, or self-neglect, no amount of success will override it. The frequency of our thoughts and beliefs shapes the vibration of our reality.

Pause & Reflect: *What repeating mental or emotional loops do I now see as conditioning rather than truth?*

The Moment Everything Changed

For me, the turning point in my life didn't come in a thunderclap.

It came on the night of July 17, 2012, when I sat alone in the quiet of my own despair and seriously considered suicide. No one knew the pain I was experiencing. From the outside, nothing looked broken. But inside, I was rapidly unraveling.

The next day, I walked into a meeting of Alcoholics Anonymous. That was my Hail Mary—if that program didn't work, I didn't have a Plan B.

That moment was the beginning of my liberation—my emotional and spiritual freedom.

It didn't happen overnight; healing rarely does. But it was in AA, where radical honesty was the word of the day—where I had no choice but to tell the truth—that I finally saw the mental cage for what it was.

And once I saw it, I knew I had to dismantle it—brick by mental brick—in order to live. Today I am grateful that I did.

Conclusion: The Truth We Must Name

The mental cage is real.
But so is the key.

You are not trapped by failure.
You are trapped by the story you tell yourself... by the story success was supposed to fulfill.

This book is your invitation to change the narrative—not by force, but by awareness.
Not by struggling or striving, but by surrendering to the work of the Self-Empowerment Breakthrough Process™—a deeply

transformative system that involves reflection, reimagining, release, reprogramming, and recreation.

In the next chapter we begin, as all deep work begins, by understanding how your mind got wired into limitation in the first place—and how you can begin to reclaim it.

Deep Dive Questions: Reclaiming My Freedom

1. In what ways have I confused success with fulfillment?
2. Where in my life do I feel confined, even if everything "looks good" on the outside?
3. What unspoken desires or truths have I silenced in order to appear competent or strong?
4. What does freedom mean to me beyond career or achievement?
5. What would it mean for me to reclaim my power—gently, consciously, and on my own terms?
6. What stories am I telling myself that are limiting, disenfranchising, or denying my inner peace?

"Freedom begins the moment you remember you are the author of your story, not a minor character in your life."
~ Dr. Sue Carter Collins

Chapter 2

The Wiring Behind the Wall – Understanding How the Brain, Mind, and Energy Systems Shape Your Life

"The mind is everything. What you think, you become."

~Buddha

Waking Up From the Dream

Most people never question the way they think. They exist in a dream-like state, assuming their thoughts are facts, their habits are hardwired, and their feelings are simply who they are. But the truth is, the way you experience reality is not fixed. It is filtered—through your brain, your mind, your emotions, and your energy.

To master your mind, you need to understand how your inner systems actually function. This chapter introduces the key players: the brain, the mind (including the subconscious and superconscious), the heart as a neurological and intuitive center, and the energy field that surrounds and animates you. By the end, you'll see that your thoughts are not random, your emotions are not irrational, and your reality is not accidental. Perhaps then, you'll commit to waking up from the dream that has shaped your existence.

The Brain: Your Predictive Operating System

The human brain isn't simply a memory bank. Neuroscientist Lisa Feldman Barrett explains that the brain is a dynamic prediction machine, processing billions of bits of information every second, most of it beneath conscious awareness. Its primary job is not to make you happy—it's to keep you alive.

To accomplish this, the brain relies heavily on prediction and pattern recognition. Philosopher and cognitive scientist Andy Clark describes this as predictive coding—the brain constantly scans for familiar cues and generates expectations about what will happen next. When its prediction matches reality, you feel a sense of control. When it doesn't, the brain interprets the mismatch as a potential threat and activates stress responses.

This is why you might feel disproportionately anxious during a new experience. Your brain is not reacting to the moment itself—it's reacting to the gap between the present and its stored prediction of danger. Because the brain is biased toward the familiar, it often reinforces even painful thought patterns simply because they are known. In other words, your brain will choose predictable discomfort over unfamiliar joy—unless you intentionally retrain it.

Pause & Reflect: Think about a time when your brain seemed to overreact—when your anxiety felt bigger than the actual situation. Was your response about the present moment, or about something familiar from your past?

The Mind: More Than the Brain

While the brain is a physical organ, the mind is broader and more elusive. It encompasses your thoughts, beliefs, memories, imagination, intentions, and self-awareness. It operates on at least three levels:

- The conscious mind handles daily thinking. Logical and analytical, it accounts for only about 5–10% of your mental activity.
- The subconscious mind runs the show behind the scenes. Biologist Bruce Lipton notes that it stores habits, emotional responses, and implicit beliefs—and drives 90–95% of behavior.
- The superconscious mind is the higher intelligence within you. It is the part of your mind that intuits, receives spiritual insight, and connects with divine wisdom beyond logic or memory.

Most mindset work stops at the conscious level. But true transformation requires engaging the subconscious and superconscious. This book is designed to help you work with all three.

The Heart Has an Intelligence of Its Own

For centuries, science regarded the heart as nothing more than a pump. But research in neurocardiology has shown that the heart contains more than 40,000 neurons capable of sensing, feeling, learning, and remembering. The HeartMath Institute describes this as the "heart brain," and its influence on the mind and emotions is profound.

Research director Rollin McCraty explains that the heart sends more signals to the brain than the brain sends to the heart. These signals regulate emotional responses, synchronize brain rhythms, and modulate hormonal activity. When you experience appreciation, compassion, or peace, your heart rhythms become coherent, positively affecting clarity, emotional balance, and decision-making.

The heart also serves as a bridge between the physical and the energetic. Many describe it as a tuning fork for intuitive wisdom. You've likely felt this when you "just knew" something in your chest before your mind caught up. That's not just emotion—it's intelligence.

Pause & Reflect: Recall a decision you "knew" in your heart before your head could explain it. How did your body signal that truth? Did you trust it—or override it with logic?

Emotions Are Signals, Not Enemies

Emotions often get dismissed as irrational or inconvenient, especially in high-performing environments. But they are neither random nor irrelevant. Emotions are energy in motion—feedback about how your current experience aligns (or misaligns) with your values and needs.

Psychopharmacologist Candace Pert demonstrated that each emotion has a biochemical signature that influences your focus, behavior, immune function, and even your capacity for empathy. Fear, for example, triggers adrenaline and cortisol. Adrenaline increases heart rate, quickens breathing, and sharpens the senses for immediate action. Cortisol sustains energy and manages inflammation for longer-term coping.

By contrast, joy and love release dopamine and oxytocin. Dopamine reinforces pleasurable experiences, making you want to repeat them. Oxytocin, the so-called "love hormone," strengthens bonds in moments of connection and care.

From a metaphysical standpoint, emotions carry vibrational frequencies. High-vibration states like love and gratitude expand your energetic field, while lower vibrations like shame and resentment contract it. Both science and spirituality affirm the same truth: your emotional state doesn't just color your experience—it creates it.

Your Energy Field: The Invisible Architecture

You are more than flesh and bone. Surrounding your body is a measurable electromagnetic field—a biofield—that holds the imprint of your thoughts, feelings, and intentions. Biophysicist James Oschman has shown that this field responds to both internal and external stimuli.

The principle is simple: energy flows where attention goes. Thoughts rooted in fear or scarcity contract your biofield and keep your nervous system locked in fight-or-flight. Thoughts grounded in trust and love expand your field—and with it, your capacity to create, connect, and heal.

Spiritual traditions call this biofield the aura, the soul light, or the divine template. Whatever the name, the truth remains: your energy precedes your presence. Others feel it. You feel it. And it is constantly being shaped by your inner state.

Pause & Reflect: Notice how your energy shifts in different environments. Where do you feel most expansive and aligned? Where do you feel contracted or drained? What might that reveal about your inner state?

Rewiring the Whole System

The brain, mind, heart, emotions, and energy field do not function in isolation. They are deeply interconnected, influencing one another in a continuous loop.

Here's how it often works:

- A triggering event activates a neural pathway in the brain.
- That pathway cues a subconscious belief or story in the mind.
- The story generates an emotional response.
- The emotion affects your heart rhythm, your energy field, and your subsequent choices.

Over time, this becomes a feedback loop. Your brain expects stress, your body feels stress, your energy attracts stress—and your life confirms the very pattern you long to escape.

Conclusion: You're Not Failing, You're Entering The Unknown

You now understand the core architecture of your inner world—and how your biology, psychology, and energy systems interact. The brain is wired to protect you, not to expand you. So when you begin to think differently or imagine a new version of your life, discomfort is natural. Resistance does not mean you're failing—it means you're entering the unknown, and the mind equates the unknown with danger.

Rewiring is not about forcing yourself into positive thinking. It is about discerning between the voice of survival and the voice of your soul. Between familiar fear and unfamiliar freedom. Between the programming that helped you endure the past and the truth that will empower your future.

But understanding alone is not enough. To create meaningful change, you must uncover the loops that keep you stuck. In the next chapter, we'll explore the power of mental loops, triggers, and emotional set points—and how to break free from the invisible patterns that sabotage growth.

Pause & Reflect

Before you move on, take a moment to notice how these systems are already at work in your life.

- When have you felt your brain defaulting to the familiar, even when you wanted change?
- How does your heart signal truth to you, even when your mind is uncertain?
- Do you notice your energy shift around certain people, environments, or thoughts?

Awareness of these patterns is not about judgment—it's about learning the unique ways your inner world communicates with you.

Deep Dive Practice: Rewiring Awareness

1. How does my brain's preference for familiarity show up in my daily habits?
2. Where do I notice emotions that seem tied to an old version of me?
3. When have I ignored my heart's wisdom, and what happened as a result?

4. How do I typically respond to the unfamiliar—with curiosity, resistance, or fear?
5. What is one practice I can adopt this week to create more coherence between my mind, heart, and energy?

"Your inner systems are not your prison—they are your portal to peace and freedom."

~Dr. Sue Carter Collins

Chapter 3

Interrupting the Pattern – How Mental Loops and Triggers Hijack Your Mind

"If you don't like the road you're walking, start paving another one."

~Dolly Parton

Getting Stuck in the Rabbit Hole

Sometimes we find ourselves thinking the same thoughts over and over again—like falling down a rabbit hole with no bottom. One thought leads to another, looping endlessly. Even when we recognize what's happening, the momentum can feel too strong to stop.

Repetitive thoughts create *mental loops* that replay like a broken record. They often start with a triggering event—someone's comment, an unexpected setback, even a fleeting glance that feels like disapproval. Suddenly, we're swept into overthinking, self-criticism, or anxiety.

The brain creates these loops as a survival mechanism. Neuroscience tells us that the brain thrives on prediction and efficiency. When something unsettling happens, it searches its database of past experiences, looking for a match. Once it finds one, it activates a learned response—often without conscious awareness. Over time, these responses harden into automatic habits of thought, shaping how we perceive both ourselves and the world.

So, What Exactly Are Mental Loops?

Mental loops form when a thought or belief gets triggered and then reinforces itself through repetition and emotional charge. Eventually, the loop becomes so ingrained that it shapes identity and behavior.

They often sound like:

- *"I should be doing more."*
- *"They don't really value me."*
- *"I always mess things up."*
- *"What if something goes wrong?"*

Each thought feeds into an emotional state—fear, shame, or doubt. With repetition, these loops carve deep grooves in the brain's neural pathways, becoming part of the *internal script* we live by. Psychologists call these *identity scripts*—subconscious narratives that dictate who we believe we are and what we're allowed to expect from life.

Pause & Reflect: What "script" do you find yourself repeating most often? Does it sound like someone else's voice, or your own?

Identity Scripts

Identity scripts often originate in childhood. They can be shaped by family dynamics, cultural expectations, or societal messages. These scripts whisper rules about our worth and identity:

- *"My value lies in how much I give."*
- *"I'm loved only when I succeed."*
- *"I can't make mistakes."*

For instance, a woman taught to equate worth with selflessness may feel guilt or anxiety whenever she sets boundaries. The script isn't her truth—it's a learned survival code. Yet, left unchecked, it becomes the lens through which she interprets her life.

The Trigger Loop: When the Past Replays Itself

A *trigger* is any stimulus—internal or external—that evokes an emotional response tied to past experience. When we are triggered, we rarely respond to the present. We react from an old wound.

Here's a brief example of how the *trigger loop* works:

1. A stimulus occurs (You receive criticism from a colleague).
2. It activates a mental loop (You think, *"I'm not good enough"*).

3. This sparks an emotional response (You feel shame, anxiety, anger, or fear).
4. That emotion drives behavior (You react by withdrawing, overcompensating, or lashing out).
5. The outcome reinforces the original belief (You think, *"See, I really don't belong here"*).

From a neuroscience perspective, this is a hijacking by the amygdala, the brain's threat detector. It fires off alarms before the rational prefrontal cortex has time to evaluate the situation. Psychiatrist Aaron Beck, founder of cognitive therapy, showed how such distorted patterns of thought fuel depression and anxiety—loops that repeat until interrupted.

Metaphysically, this is explained by the **Law of Resonance**: the emotional frequency you vibrate at is the frequency you attract and perceive. If your dominant state is fear, you'll unconsciously filter reality in ways that confirm fear. You won't see the admiration—you'll zero in on the one critique.

Pause & Reflect: Think of a recent trigger. Did your reaction belong to the present moment—or to an older version of you?

The Emotional Set Point

Each of us carries an *emotional set point*—a baseline state we tend to return to. Shaped by early environment, trauma, and repeated patterns, this baseline influences how we interpret life.

- A high set point (trust, curiosity, calm) leads us to perceive challenges as manageable.
- A low set point (fear, resentment, overwhelm) makes even neutral events feel threatening.

The set point interacts with the trigger loop. The lower your baseline, the faster you are hijacked. The higher your baseline, the more space you create between stimulus and response. Practices like meditation, breathwork, and journaling help recalibrate this set point toward greater peace.

How Thoughts Become Things

Mental loops don't stay in the mind—they manifest in reality.

Here's the chain:

- Repeated thoughts strengthen neural pathways.
- Neural pathways become mental habits.
- Mental habits shape emotions.
- Emotions create vibrational frequencies.
- Frequencies influence what we attract, notice, and create.

Neuroplasticity research confirms this. Psychiatrist Aaron Beck demonstrated that repetitive negative thoughts reinforce the very networks that generate them. Similarly, Norman Doidge, in *The Brain That Changes Itself*, showed that conscious repetition of new thoughts and practices can rewire the brain.

Metaphysics frames this simply: thought + emotion = creation. Every affirmation, visualization, or gratitude practice has the power to shift both brain wiring and energetic vibration—reshaping reality from the inside out.

Interrupting the Pattern

You can't always stop the first thought or prevent a trigger. But you can learn to *interrupt the loop* before it runs unchecked.

This begins with awareness—observing thoughts without judgment, noticing emotional responses, and pausing before reacting. Practices like mindfulness, breathwork, and somatic awareness create a vital gap between stimulus and response.

In that gap lies power. Each pause provides a chance for you to choose differently. Over time, these interruptions form new neural pathways. And those new pathways become the scaffolding of a new identity—one rooted in freedom, not in fear.

Conclusion: You Can Rewrite the Script

Mental loops, emotional triggers, and identity scripts are not life sentences. They are programs in your subconscious mind that can be rewritten. True power begins with this awareness. When you finally recognize the pattern, you can reclaim the choice to step outside of it.

In the next chapter, we'll explore how belief systems are formed—how subconscious stories become blueprints for decisions and identity—and how to begin rewriting them.

Deep Dive Practice: Interrupting My Loops

1. What mental loop do I recognize as most active in my life?
2. What emotion tends to surface when I'm triggered, and where might it have originated?
3. Can I recall a recent moment where I reacted rather than responded? What choice might I make next time?
4. Which identity script am I most ready to release?
5. What new emotional baseline do I want to cultivate moving forward?

"Awareness is the first act of power. Once you see the loop, you no longer have to live inside it."
~Dr. Sue Carter Collins

Chapter 4

Mind Scripts – The Hidden System Beneath Your Thoughts

"The subconscious mind is the seat of memory, habit, instinct, and automatic mental action. It is the medium through which thought becomes law."

~Ernest Holmes

Your Beliefs Run the Show—Even If You Don't Know It

Beliefs are not born. They are built.
And most of them are built before you know you have a choice.

From the moment you're born, your brain is absorbing data. You're not just taking in facts—you're taking in meaning. You're learning who to trust, how to behave, whether you matter, and what is safe. These early perceptions form the blueprint of your life. They become the lens through which you interpret everything—and the scaffolding of the identity you will unconsciously construct.

Beliefs don't just live in your mind. They live in your nervous system, your emotional responses, and your energetic field. They shape what you notice. What you expect. What you attract. What you tolerate. Until they are brought into conscious awareness, they will quietly run the show—creating a life that you do or do not want.

From Impression to Installation: The Programming Pathway

Most of your core beliefs were not consciously chosen. They were imprinted during the earliest, most impressionable years of your life. From birth through around age seven, your brain operates primarily in theta wave states—frequencies that are highly receptive and hypnotic in nature. In this state, children absorb information directly into the subconscious without filtering it through logic or critical thought. You weren't reasoning—you were just recording.

During this formative stage, your subconscious mind acts like wet cement, ready to be inscribed by repetition, emotion, and environment. The repeated messages, modeled behaviors, and emotional tones of your early environment become the scripts you live by. Because these patterns were formed before the development of critical reasoning, they tend to be accepted as fact—not just a belief, but the truth.

Pause & Reflect:

- What early phrases or family "rules" still echo in your mind today?
- Do you ever catch yourself repeating something you heard as a child—even if you don't agree with it?

Pre-Birth Imprinting and Soul Memory

Emerging research in prenatal psychology reveals that imprinting may begin even earlier than we once thought. Fetuses respond to maternal stress, voice, music, and emotional tone. Studies show that newborns prefer stories read to them in utero. Epigenetic science further suggests that emotional imprinting and stress responses can be encoded biologically before birth.

Metaphysical traditions have long supported this view. In Eastern spirituality, this is referred to as *samskara*—imprints of past life experiences or karmic patterns. New Thought teachers describe the soul as carrying its own divine blueprint, memory, and evolutionary agenda.

Whether you view belief formation through the lens of neuroscience, prenatal psychology, or soul memory, the conclusion is the same: You arrive here influenced by forces—both seen and unseen—before you speak your first word.

The Origins of Personal Beliefs

If a child is repeatedly told they are too sensitive, too loud, or too much, those messages don't remain as simple memories—they become internalized beliefs. Likewise, if a child grows up witnessing silence, shame, control, or emotional withdrawal, they may unconsciously encode those experiences as "normal."

This results in beliefs like:

- I have to earn love.
- I'm not safe unless I'm in control.
- My needs don't matter.
- If I show up fully, I'll be rejected.

These aren't just thoughts. They are survival strategies rooted in adaptation. But what began as protection often becomes a prison. Left unchallenged, these mind scripts become default assumptions—ones that govern your life quietly and relentlessly.

Pause & Reflect:

- Which old messages about love, safety, or worth still shape the way you show up today?
- Were these truly *yours*—or inherited scripts you never chose?

Where Beliefs Live

Beliefs are not confined to the mind. They also live in the body and the energy field.

Here's a way to think about it:

- The mind holds the story.
- The body holds the memory.
- The energy field holds the frequency.

Somatic psychology confirms that trauma and emotion are stored in the body. For example, a person who holds the belief *"I am not enough"* might experience tightness in the chest, shallow breath, or a tendency to shrink in posture.

The human energy field, also known as the biofield, stores these imprints as well. Researchers have demonstrated that the electromagnetic field around the body reflects emotional and cognitive patterns. Your dominant beliefs emit a vibrational signal—one that influences how others perceive you and how you engage with life.

A Personal Story: The Hidden Belief That Almost Broke Me

I don't know exactly when it started, but at some point, I began to tell myself that I was stuck. Although I wanted to leave the university, I told myself I couldn't go anywhere else. Who would hire me?

Even though I had passed multiple advanced statistics courses during my doctoral program, I held a core belief that I wasn't good with numbers. I told myself that being a socio-legal qualitative researcher in a stats-driven world meant I would never be enough.

I didn't talk about it. Instead, I masked my fear with noble language: *I'm choosing a simpler life.* But deep down, I knew I had given up— resigned to a belief that I was inadequate.

It took years to successfully challenge that belief. Years to realize that it wasn't my truth—it was just another wound that I needed to heal. It wasn't until I reflected on my childhood that I remembered there was a time when I had been very good with numbers. In fact, I had been one of the top students in my Algebra classes. But when I transitioned to a white high school, and experienced the hostilities that accompanied desegregation, that changed. I began to question my abilities and my worth. Despite my subsequent accomplishments, this belief continued to exist at the subconscious level; controlling my thoughts and dictating my actions.

Such is the hidden power of the subconscious mind.

Pause & Reflect:

- Can you identify one "hidden belief" that has silently dictated your choices?
- How does that belief still echo in your body or energy today?

Why This Matters for Mind Mastery

Mind mastery is not about policing your thoughts. It's about understanding where they come from.

If you don't know what you believe, you can't change what you experience.
If you don't examine the blueprint, you'll keep building the same reality.
When you start to question your mind scripts—those inherited, installed, or created in response to pain—you take the first step toward freedom.

You stop living in the shadows of old narratives.
You begin to design your life from truth—not trauma.

Conclusion: Emotional Intelligence and Belief Awareness

One of the most powerful tools you can develop in the process of mind mastery is emotional intelligence (EQ)—the ability to perceive, understand, and regulate your own emotions and those of others.

Why does this matter? Because beliefs are emotionally encoded. If you can't recognize the emotional undercurrent of a thought, you can't trace it back to its source. EQ helps you become fluent in the language of your nervous system and the frequency of your thoughts. It gives you the capacity to witness what you're feeling without collapsing into it—and to rewrite the beliefs that no longer serve you.

We'll explore emotional mastery more deeply in Part III but, for now, remember:

Your beliefs are not who you are.

They are learned.
Which means they can be unlearned.

As you deepen this awareness, you'll begin to notice that not all thoughts originate from truth. Some are echoes—old internalized voices that once tried to keep you safe but now keep you small. In the next chapter, we'll meet these voices of the *Inner Critic* and uncover how they formed, why they persist, and how to reclaim your authority from them. Because once you recognize the voice that's been running the show, you can finally choose a different narrator.

Deep Dive Practice: Making the Invisible Visible

1. What beliefs were you taught (explicitly or implicitly) in your childhood about love, safety, worth, or success?
2. Which of these beliefs still shape your choices—even if you no longer agree with them?
3. Identify a "mind script" you're ready to rewrite.
4. Where in your body do you feel the weight of an old belief? What might it be telling you?
5. What new belief could you choose today that would open the door to greater freedom?

"Your beliefs form the blueprint and your awareness empowers you to rebuild your life."
~Dr. Sue Carter Collins

Chapter 5

The Inner Critic and the Ego's Game of Control

"There is nothing more important to true growth than realizing that you are not the voice of the mind—you are the one who hears it."

~Michael A. Singer

Stop Feeding the Inner Critic

There's a voice inside your mind that isn't your intuition—but it often masquerades as wisdom.

It questions your decisions, second-guesses your worth, and measures your value through comparison, productivity, or perfection. It keeps score. It whispers fears. And it sounds very convincing.

This is your inner critic—the mental gatekeeper that formed to keep you "safe" but often keeps you stuck. It is fueled by one of the most complex and misunderstood aspects of the psyche: the ego. In this chapter, you'll learn how to interrupt the energetic flow and stop feeding it.

What Is the Inner Critic, Really?

The inner critic is not a flaw in your system. It is a protective mechanism—constructed in moments when you felt unsafe, unworthy, or unseen. Its origin is often tied to early childhood years when you internalized cues about love, approval, and survival.

At some point, your subconscious determined that self-correction was safer than external rejection. If you criticized yourself before others did, maybe it wouldn't hurt as much. If you shrank before being judged, maybe you could avoid abandonment.

So the ego's voice developed, mimicking the tone of early caregivers, cultural expectations, or authority figures. Over time, it became familiar. Unchecked, it becomes law—quietly dictating your confidence, relationships, ambitions, and sense of worth.

From a neurological standpoint, the inner critic is linked to the brain's default mode network (DMN)—a system responsible for self-referential thought, mental rumination, and the replaying of past scenarios. The DMN becomes especially active when you're not focused externally, causing your mind to loop on fears, judgments, and imagined consequences.

To be clear, this voice is not your highest wisdom. It is unhealed fear in disguise.

Pause & Reflect:

- When you hear that critical voice, whose tone does it resemble?
- Do you recognize moments when it sounds like someone from your past?

Understanding the Role of the Ego

The ego is not your enemy; it is the identity structure you've built to function in the world. Its job is to protect your self-concept—even if that concept is limiting or painful.

The ego says things like:

- *"I am what I do."*
- *"I am how others see me."*
- *"I am what I control."*

The ego prefers certainty, even if that certainty is rooted in struggle. When you attempt to grow, the ego often interprets that growth as a threat. It perceives change not as transformation, but as annihilation.

As Eckhart Tolle teaches, the ego thrives on identification—with roles, wounds, drama, and survival. It operates best in the known. So when you begin to shift into unfamiliar territory, the ego panics. That's when the inner critic's voice gets really loud.

When you try to rest, the voice accuses you of being lazy. When you assert yourself, it warns that you're "too much."

When you take up space, it cautions that others will judge you.

The inner critic's voice is rarely rooted in present truth. It is often just a replay of past experiences shrouded in present fear.

Archetypes of the Inner Critic

Psychologists and spiritual teachers alike have observed that the inner critic rarely shows up in just one form. Hal and Sidra Stone (creators of *Voice Dialogue*) describe it as a "sub-personality," while other therapeutic models outline common types such as the Perfectionist or the Taskmaster. Drawing on these foundations, I've expanded the framework into what I call Surface Archetypes and Deeper Root Archetypes.

This approach helps us recognize not only the voices we hear most often, but also the deeper emotional wounds that fuel them. When you read through these archetypes, notice if any feel familiar. You may see yourself in more than one—that's normal. The point is not to label yourself, but to understand the patterns you've unconsciously carried so that you can release their grip.

Surface Archetypes

Surface archetypes are the more obvious "voices" of the critic. They operate on the front lines of your daily thoughts, shaping how you evaluate yourself in work, relationships, and personal growth. While they appear different, they all share the same goal: to keep you safe by controlling how you show up in the world.

- **The Perfectionist** – This archetype constantly demands flawlessness, insisting that if you make a single mistake, everything will collapse. It often develops in childhood environments where love and approval were conditional—based more on achievement than authenticity.
- **The Taskmaster** – This voice drives you relentlessly, telling you to push harder, work longer, and never rest. It equates value with productivity and often leads to burnout.
- **The Inner Parent** – Echoing the critical tone of a caregiver, teacher, or authority figure, this archetype disguises judgment as guidance. It sounds like protection but feels like rejection.
- **The People-Pleaser** – This one sacrifices authenticity to avoid conflict or rejection. It equates harmony with safety, even at the cost of your truth.
- **The Shape-Shifter** – This archetype changes who you are depending on the environment. You may blend in so well that you lose sight of your real identity.
- **The Over-Achiever** – This one convinces you that your worth is measured by accolades and external validation. No matter how much you accomplish, it never feels like enough.
- **The Hidden Visionary** – This voice buries your brilliance out of fear of being judged or misunderstood. It insists invisibility is safer than being seen.

Deeper Root Archetypes

Beneath the surface lies something more powerful: the deeper root archetypes. These are the emotional blueprints that formed in childhood and still echo through your adult life. Where the surface archetypes dictate behavior, the deeper root archetypes reveal the underlying wounds. When you understand them, you realize the critic's voice is not random—it is a direct reflection of your earliest conditioning.

- **The Abandoned Child** – She believes love must always be earned and lives with a constant fear of being left behind. Her strategies are over-compliance, over-performance, and self-sacrifice. She is driven by a desperate need to prove she is worthy of staying.
- **The Healer** – She feels responsible for everyone else's happiness and neglects her own needs in the process. Her worth is tied to how much she can give, fix, or rescue. While she appears strong, underneath lies the fear that she won't be loved if she stops caretaking.
- **The Rebel** – Outwardly, she resists structure, authority, or rules, projecting strength and independence. But beneath the defiance lies an unprocessed fear of control, rejection, or unworthiness. Her rebellion is not always empowerment—it is often self-protection.
- **The Controller** – She tries to orchestrate everything to prevent vulnerability or emotional exposure. She equates surrender with danger, so she clings tightly to power—even when that control robs her of peace and intimacy.

Pause & Reflect

Take a moment to notice which voices sound most familiar to you.

- Which surface archetypes show up most often in your daily self-talk?
- Which deeper root archetype feels like it has shaped your story the most?
- How does it feel to realize that these voices are not your truth, but protective roles you once needed to survive?

You may want to jot down your reflections before moving on. Awareness is the first step in releasing their control.

Why We Believe the Critic

The inner critic is effective because it borrows from your past. It blends fragments of truth with distortion and presents them in your own voice. That's why it feels so real.

It draws upon childhood experiences, cultural conditioning, and trauma. The moment someone shamed you, the day you failed, the season you felt abandoned—your subconscious stored those experiences and built a defense system around them. When the critic speaks, it is pulling directly from that archive.

From a psychological perspective, this is confirmation bias in action. Your brain seeks evidence to confirm what it already believes. If you think you're not enough, your mind will highlight every flaw, every rejection, every moment of weakness—while filtering out praise and success.

Metaphysically, Florence Scovel Shinn described this as the law of your subconscious: what you hold as true becomes the law of your life. The inner critic is dangerous because it projects your past into your future, turning fear into expectation.

The critic doesn't just whisper; it rehearses.
It isn't truth—it's trauma trying to repeat itself.

Pause & Reflect:

- When your critic speaks, what past event does it echo?
- Can you see how it might be projecting that past into your present?

How To Reclaim Your Inner Authority

You cannot defeat the inner critic by silencing it. But you can reclaim your authority over it.

Step 1: Identify the Voice

- Notice the specific phrases it repeats.
- Ask: *When did this voice first appear? Whose tone does it echo? Is it speaking truth or rehearsing fear?*
- Recognize that it's not your intuition—it's fear masquerading as truth.

Step 2: Interrupt the Pattern

- Pause when the critic speaks.
- Name it out loud: *"That's my critic, not my truth."*
- Create distance by labeling: *"This is an old script, not my present reality."*

Step 3: Integrate With Compassion

Instead of fighting the critic, acknowledge its intention: protection. Then release its control.

- Say: *"Thank you for trying to keep me safe. But that's an old script. I choose differently now."*
- Replace with affirmations aligned to truth: *"I am safe to be seen. I am worthy without proving. I am free to grow."*

This is not about ego death. It's about ego integration. Your goal is not to eliminate your ego, but to liberate your identity from harmful, fear-driven patterns so your authentic self can lead.

Why This Matters for Mind Mastery

Mind mastery is not about eliminating fear—it's about refusing to obey fear disguised as truth.

The inner critic is one of the ego's strongest tools of control. It uses your past to lock you out of your future. But your mind isn't meant to be a prison—it's meant to be a field of creation.

When you stop giving the critic control, you allow your true self to take over. You stop fueling the loop of shame and self-doubt. You stop replaying inherited narratives of "not enough." And you begin to create space for new thought, new energy, and new possibility.

You don't have to prove the critic wrong. You only have to stop letting it speak for you and living by its rules.

Conclusion: You're the Controller of Your Destiny

Mind mastery is the practice of discerning which voices to amplify and which to release. The inner critic is not your truth—it is your training. It is the voice of past pain, outdated protection, and inherited fear. But you're no longer the child who had to shrink. You're no longer the woman who had to earn her worth through perfection.

Now, you are the architect of your thoughts and the controller of your destiny. Your power is not in silencing the voice but in no longer allowing it to speak for you.

As you quiet the noise of the inner critic, a deeper realization begins to emerge: those voices were never yours alone. They were shaped by family, culture, religion, and society—by invisible programs that began long before you knew you were being indoctrinated.

In the next chapter, we'll trace the origin of those inner voices back to the cultural, familial, and societal conditioning that taught you who to be—and uncover how those subconscious patterns formed your belief system. You can't fully reclaim your freedom until you understand what has been shaping it.

Deep Dive Practice: It's All In Your Mind

1. What does your inner critic say most often? What phrases or beliefs show up repeatedly?
2. Whose voice does your critic echo from your past?
3. Which archetype or root archetype feels most familiar to you?
4. What is your critic trying to protect you from—and what truth does your higher self know instead?
5. If your inner critic no longer had power, how would your life look and feel different?

"Freedom begins the moment you stop mistaking the echoes of your past for the voice of your truth."
~Dr. Sue Carter Collins

Chapter 6

The Cost of Conditioning – What's Really Holding You Back

*"The world programmed you before you had
the power to choose.
But now that you do, it's time to become the
author of your own story."*

~Dr. Sue Carter Collins

Is That Really You?

You've been told who you are since the day you arrived.
Not always in words.
Sometimes in glances.
Sometimes in absence.
Sometimes in silence.

You've been shaped by rules you didn't create.
By beliefs you never consciously agreed to.
By systems and stories that began long before you did.

This is conditioning—the inherited and absorbed mental programming that forms the foundation of your identity. It is not inherently bad but it is incomplete.

Until you see it clearly, it will quietly govern your thoughts, emotions, and behavior. It will shape the lens through which you perceive life—and, even worse—distort how you see yourself.

Now that you are an adult you get to choose.
Is that really you?

Pause & Reflect: Think about one label or role that others placed on you early in life. Do you still carry it? If so, does it feel authentic—or does it feel like a mask you've outgrown?

So, What Is Conditioning?

Conditioning is the accumulation of subconscious patterns shaped by repetition, reward, exposure, and emotional intensity. These patterns become ingrained through early childhood experiences—particularly during stages when the brain is most impressionable.

From birth to age seven, a child's dominant brainwave state is theta—a deeply absorbent, hypnotic state in which beliefs, habits, and identity constructs are formed without the filter of conscious analysis. Dr. Bruce Lipton, author of *The Biology of Belief*, refers to this as the "programming phase," in which the subconscious mind is shaped by environmental input, especially from parents, authority figures, and social surroundings.

Developmental psychologist Dr. Daniel Siegel adds that during this phase, children rely on "interpersonal neurobiology" to wire their brains through attachment and relational experiences. In other words, the way we are treated shapes not only what we believe—but how our nervous system functions.

Conditioning includes multiple layers:

- **Familial Conditioning** – Inherited messages passed down generationally.
- **Cultural and Societal Conditioning** – Norms based on race, gender, religion, class, sexuality, and social status.
- **Educational and Religious Conditioning** – Ideologies taught as absolute truth before discernment developed.
- **Trauma-Based Conditioning** – Protective responses formed in moments of emotional pain or neglect.

These messages become encoded not just in your thoughts—but in your body, your nervous system, and your energy field. Over time, they form the foundation of your perceived self.

But they are not your truth.
They are the template of who you were taught to be.

The Hidden Cost of Living From Conditioning

Living from outdated conditioning is like running a high-performance computer with corrupted software. It may function—but it can't evolve.

Emotionally, it breeds confusion, shame, and self-abandonment.

Energetically, it restricts your flow and expression.

Spiritually, it blocks alignment with your divine identity.

In metaphysical terms, conditioning forms an energetic distortion between your soul and your experience. In the teachings of Ernest Holmes and Joel Goldsmith, the subconscious becomes a creative filter through which Infinite Mind flows. If the filter is clouded with false beliefs, then your outer reality will mirror that distortion. The cost is not just inner conflict—it's misalignment with your divine potential.

Pause & Reflect: Where do you notice the tension between who you feel called to be and who you were conditioned to be? Write down one way this tension shows up in your daily life.

How Conditioning Shows Up

You'll know conditioning is running the show when you feel guilty resting—even when you're exhausted. When you downplay your truth to avoid being seen as "too much." When you sabotage opportunities right before success arrives. When you avoid setting boundaries in fear of rejection. When you shrink in rooms where your presence is needed most.

These aren't personality flaws. They're patterned outcomes of unexamined programming.

From a neuroscience perspective, conditioned responses are maintained through neural pathways that have been strengthened by repeated thought and behavior. These pathways become mental "defaults" until new, conscious circuits are formed through neuroplasticity—a process that requires both awareness and repetition.

Conditioning and the Nervous System

Conditioning is not just mental—it is somatic. It lives in the body and nervous system. When a child is repeatedly told to behave, to suppress emotion, or to minimize needs, the nervous system encodes safety as self-silencing. Over time, the body becomes the blueprint for survival, not wholeness.

This is why many adults find themselves living in chronic states that don't match present reality. Hypervigilance develops when the nervous system is trained to always be on guard. You become constantly alert, scanning for threats, never able to fully relax, because your body has been wired to expect harm. Anxiety emerges when the nervous system normalizes tension, leaving you in a heightened state of arousal, with racing thoughts and a constant anticipation of worst-case scenarios. Even peace can feel suspicious.

In other cases, the body moves into freeze or numbing. Here, the system shuts down to avoid emotional overload, leaving you stuck, disconnected, or unable to feel joy even in moments that should be fulfilling. Over-responsibility is another common imprint. It shows up as the compulsion to take care of everyone else, fix situations, and prevent conflict at all costs. You begin to confuse responsibility with love and control with safety, even when those strategies leave you drained and unfulfilled.

Healing requires more than positive thinking. It requires retraining the nervous system to recognize that joy, rest, intimacy, and expansion are not threats—they are birthrights. Somatic therapies, breathwork, meditation, trauma-informed movement, and energy healing are powerful tools in this recalibration.

Pause & Reflect: When your body goes into stress mode, what is your most common default—hypervigilance, anxiety, shutdown, or over-responsibility? How does this pattern limit your freedom?

The Role of Archetypes and Assigned Roles

In Chapter 5, we explored how the inner critic shows up as a voice. Conditioning operates differently. Instead of speaking, it scripts you into roles—identities you were often assigned before you had the power to choose.

One of the most common is the **Good Girl** or **Nice Guy**, shaped by the expectation to always be agreeable and avoid conflict. Love feels earned by being easy to handle, even if that means silencing your true feelings. The **Caregiver** role is another, where you feel responsible for the well-being of others while consistently neglecting your own needs. In this identity, self-sacrifice becomes a currency for worth, and you learn to believe that being needed is the only way to stay loved.

The **Achiever** is the role built on performance. In this script, identity revolves around accomplishment, rest feels like laziness, and success becomes the only acceptable proof of value. Then there is the **Invisible One**, who learned that safety came through staying small. Needs, presence, and dreams are minimized, not because they don't exist, but because being unseen once felt like the only way to avoid judgment or punishment. Finally, the **Fixer** emerges— the one who takes on the emotional weight of others, solving their problems in order to feel valuable. This role often masks unhealed wounds, using caretaking as a distraction from personal pain.

Each of these roles was born from a need for safety in environments that could not hold your full authenticity. They may have helped you survive, but they were never meant to define who you are.

Pause & Reflect: Which of these roles feels most familiar to you? The Good Girl, the Caregiver, the Achiever, the Invisible One, or the Fixer? What would change in your life if you no longer had to play that part?

Why This Matters for Mind Mastery

You cannot master your mind if you don't understand who programmed it.

Mind mastery requires you to become the observer and architect of your mental landscape. It invites you to unlearn the lies, question the assumptions, and choose your beliefs with intention.

This is not about blaming your parents, your culture, or your past. It's about becoming aware of what you've inherited—so you can consciously decide what to keep and what to release.

Each time you choose your truth over your training, you reclaim your sovereignty.
Each time you shed an inherited identity, you create space for your divine one.

You weren't born to obey a script.
You were born to rewrite the narrative.

Conclusion: Reclaim Your Mind

Reclaiming your mind from the grip of conditioning is not an act of rebellion—it is an act of self-honoring. When you begin to witness the inherited beliefs, roles, and nervous system patterns that have shaped you, you return to your power as a conscious creator.

Mind mastery begins not with control, but with awareness. From that awareness, the possibility of redefinition becomes real—as you see it, you can shift it. You are not bound by who you were taught to be. You are free to remember who you truly are.

In the chapters ahead, we'll take this awareness and turn it into transformation. You've uncovered the old patterns—now it's time to learn how to overwrite them. In the next chapter, you'll be introduced to **The Mind Mastery Solution™**, a multidimensional framework that unites science, psychology, and spirituality to create lasting change from the inside out. Because awareness is only the beginning—what you do with that awareness is where the real power lies.

Deep Dive Practice: It's Time to Uninstall the Program

1. What beliefs did you inherit that you've never truly questioned?
2. What roles or labels were placed on you as a child? Do they still serve you?
3. In what ways have you traded authenticity for belonging or approval?
4. Where in your life are you still living according to rules that don't reflect your truth?
5. What conditioned patterns show up in your nervous system—anxiety, over-responsibility, emotional shutdown?
6. What would it feel like to make choices from alignment rather than programming?

"Just because it feels familiar doesn't mean it's your truth.
Love yourself enough to choose again."
~Dr. Sue Carter Collins

Understanding the Terrain of the Mind

The first six chapters of this journey have laid the foundational groundwork for transformation. Together, we've peeled back the layers of mental conditioning to reveal the powerful—but often hidden—forces shaping how we think, feel, and live.

You now understand that the mind is not simply a thinking organ. It is a landscape; a multidimensional field influenced by biology, beliefs, brainwave states, nervous system patterns, energetic imprints, and early social conditioning. Until we become conscious of this terrain, we are destined to walk the same circular path—repeating patterns that were never truly ours to begin with.

So, let's recap the most vital insights from Part I:

The Brain is Wired for Survival—Not Expansion.
The brain's default programming favors familiarity over growth. It is designed to protect you, not propel you. Left unexamined, it will resist change in favor of staying "safe," even when that safety is rooted in suffering.

The Mind Has Layers—And Most of Them Are Subconscious.
Your conscious mind may set intentions, but it's the subconscious—shaped by childhood imprinting, trauma, repetition, and energetic exposure—that determines your emotional set point, beliefs, and behaviors. Above both is the superconscious: the field of divine intelligence whispering who you're here to become.

Beliefs Are Not Truths—They're Instructions.
What you consistently think, feel, and expect becomes the code that governs your experience. Beliefs are not facts. They are learned, rehearsed, absorbed—and they can be reprogrammed through awareness and repetition.

The Inner Critic Isn't Wisdom—It's Wounded Protection.
That voice in your head that doubts your worth or shames your desire is not your highest self speaking. It is the voice of fear, shaped by your past, masquerading as logic. It often reflects the roles you were conditioned to play and the pain you've yet to release.

Your Identity Isn't Fixed—It's Programmable.
You are not a product of fate. You are a product of programming—and that programming can be rewritten. Your identity is elastic, not permanent. It can be redefined through conscious awareness, intentional thought, emotional alignment, and spiritual remembrance.

Energy Matters—Because You Are Energy.
Thoughts are electric, emotions are magnetic, and together they set the energetic tone of your life. Every belief you carry sends a signal into the field around you. Mind mastery is not just mental—it's also energetic, requiring coherence between thought, feeling, and action.

The Cost of Unconscious Conditioning is Self-Abandonment.
Inherited roles, cultural expectations, and subconscious scripts may have once helped you survive—but they now keep you stuck. The price of unconscious conditioning is your authenticity, your joy, your purpose. The moment you recognize that the script isn't yours, you have the power to rewrite it.

Pause & Reflect: As you sit with these insights, which one feels most alive for you right now? Where do you already see its truth showing up in your own life—and how might your awareness of it change what you choose next?

Conclusion: Moving Beyond Insight Into Transformation

As you've seen, the mind is powerful—and without mastery, it often becomes a silent architect of limitation. Now that you understand how your thoughts, beliefs, and emotional patterns have been shaped—and how they shape your reality—it's time to move beyond insight into transformation.

As we close this first part of our journey, take a breath and acknowledge how far you've come in understanding the landscape of your own mind. In Part II, you'll be introduced to the Mind Mastery Solution™—the framework that turns awareness into action. At its heart lies the Self-Empowerment Breakthrough Process™ (SEB Process™), a powerful five-phase journey that bridges reflection and embodiment. It's here that understanding becomes transformation and knowledge becomes lived experience.

Awareness awakens the path.

Action walks it.

Mastery lives it.

---

*"Once you've seen the program, you no longer
have to be the puppet. Awareness is the beginning
of personal freedom."*

~Dr. Sue Carter Collins

PART II

The Self-Empowerment Breakthrough Process

Now that you understand the architecture of the mind, it's time to rebuild from within. In this section, you'll move through the five transformative phases of the Self-Empowerment Breakthrough Process™—Reflecting, Reimagining, Releasing, Reprogramming, and Recreating.

Each phase brings you closer to the truth of who you are, guiding you from insight to embodiment, from knowing to being.

Here, healing becomes design, and alignment becomes a lived practice. This is the sacred work of rewiring your inner world so that your outer life reflects your highest truth.

Chapter 7

The Mind Mastery Solution™ – A New Framework for Lasting Change

"You can't change what you refuse to confront.
But once you become conscious,
you become powerful."

~Dr. Sue Carter Collins

A Note Before We Begin

This chapter is different from those that came before it. Unlike the reflective explorations of Part I, this section functions as a roadmap—a methodology you'll carry with you through the rest of the book. Think of it as your orientation: the big picture of how transformation unfolds, step by step. You may not need to pause for reflection here as you did earlier, but do read with attentiveness. What you learn in this chapter will be the compass that guides every practice, story, and insight that follows.

Life Reimagined

Welcome to Part II of your journey—the pivot point where insight merges with implementation. Where the groundwork laid through awareness and reflection begins to crystallize into a repeatable method for lasting transformation.

This chapter is the bridge between your "aha moments" and your actual breakthroughs. It introduces the methodology that will guide the remainder of this book and serve as the foundation for how you create sustainable, soul-aligned change.

What Is the Mind Mastery Solution™?

The Mind Mastery Solution™ is a comprehensive framework that integrates neuroscience, metaphysics, psychology, and spiritual embodiment. It is designed to help high-achieving women like you rewire disempowering thought patterns, reclaim authentic power, and live from a place of intentional truth.

It rests on three core principles:

1. You are not your past conditioning.
2. You can consciously rewire how you think, feel, and respond.
3. Transformation becomes sustainable when you align mind, energy, and identity.

This framework draws from four intersecting disciplines:

- Neuroscience focuses on how neural pathways form and how to interrupt and replace them.
- Metaphysics examines how consciousness, belief, and energy shape reality.

- Energy psychology explores how vibration and emotion influence health and behavior.
- Embodied spirituality delves into how lasting change is anchored in the body and nervous system, not just the mind.

You'll notice this is not just a method. It is a multidimensional approach to human transformation—one that honors both science and soul.

Introducing the SEB Process™

At the heart of the Mind Mastery Solution is the Self-Empowerment Breakthrough Process™, or SEB Process™—a five-phase transformation method that mirrors the nonlinear, layered nature of healing and evolution.

Unlike surface-level tools or one-size-fits-all coaching strategies, the SEB Process is sacred, adaptive, and somatically aware. It honors that true change doesn't happen through logic alone—it must occur at the level of identity, belief, emotion, energy, and embodiment.

The Five Phases of the SEB Process™:

Phase 1: Reflection
In this phase you become conscious of your current programming. This includes the internal narratives, belief systems, and behavioral patterns that have shaped your results—and the emotional and energetic triggers behind them.

Phase 2: Reimagining

This phase focuses on the activation of possibility. You are encouraged to Dream Big—to envision who you are becoming, beyond your conditioning. You give language, image, and energetic resonance to your next-level self.

Phase 3: Releasing

This phase embodies the transformation gap. Here, you let go—emotionally, cognitively, and energetically—of outdated roles, inherited beliefs, survival patterns, and inner burdens that no longer align with your truth.

Phase 4: Reprogramming

This phase is all about encoding new patterns. Using repetition, visualization, somatic reinforcement, and spiritual principles, you begin to install new beliefs, behaviors, and identity-based scripts that reflect your true self.

Phase 5: Recreation

This is the embodiment phase. Here, you live from the new paradigm. Your thoughts, choices, presence, and energy reflect your empowered self—not perfectly, but consistently and consciously.

The Slinky Analogy: Why Transformation Isn't Linear

Unlike many self-help systems that promote a step-by-step linear ascent, the SEB Process recognizes that transformation is spiral-shaped. You might think of it like a slinky moving upward and downward at the same time. The deeper you go in reflection, the greater the likelihood of your transformation.

Each time you return to a familiar pattern, you're not starting over. You're simply revisiting it from a higher frequency—with more awareness, maturity, and self-trust. This looping is not regression—it is high-level refinement.

This model incorporates neuroplasticity (the brain's ability to rewire through experience), metaphysical law (the universe responds to vibration, not perfection), and spiritual enlightenment (a chance to deepen your relationship with Source).

Why the SEB Process Works

The SEB Process is effective because it addresses the five core domains of human transformation:

1. Mental – Thought patterns, self-talk, decision filters
2. Emotional – Triggers, trauma residues, nervous system regulation
3. Energetic – Frequency, coherence, magnetic alignment
4. Behavioral – Habits, rituals, relational patterns
5. Spiritual – Identity, soul alignment, divine remembrance

Each of these layers interacts. Change one and you create momentum across all, but true and lasting change occurs when they are addressed together, not in isolation.

The SEB Process isn't a one-time event. It becomes a lifelong tool—a sacred spiral that you'll want to return to again and again, each time stepping into deeper levels of sovereignty and alignment.

What Comes Next

In the chapters that follow, we'll walk through each of the five SEB phases in depth. These are not just abstract concepts—they are embodied practices, informed by science, soul, and lived experience. You'll discover how to:

- Identify and shift disempowering stories
- Clarify your vision beyond old roles and limitations
- Let go of what no longer serves your becoming
- Rewire your mind with empowered beliefs and rituals
- Embody your divine identity in everyday life

The goal here is not to become someone new.
It is to remember and reclaim the fullness of who you've always been.

Now that you understand the structure of transformation, it's time to *experience* it. In the next chapter, we begin with **Phase 1 – Reflection**, the sacred act of seeing yourself clearly, honoring your story, and reclaiming the truth of who you've always been.
Because what you don't own will continue to own you—
and what you're willing to face, you can finally release.

"You are not here to chase change. You are here to remember your power, reclaim your truth, and realign with the design encoded in your soul. The process begins now."
~Dr. Sue Carter Collins

Chapter 8

Phase 1: Reflection – The Sacred Act of Seeing Yourself Clearly

"Clarity doesn't come from thinking harder—it comes from seeing deeper. Reflection is the moment you stop running and meet yourself at the mirror of truth."

~Dr. Sue Carter Collins

You Were Divinely Created

Before you can change your life, you must be willing to look at it. Not just the highlight reel. Not just the moments you've learned to explain away. But the undercurrent—the patterns, the pain, the programming that quietly directs your choices.

Reflection is not passive. It is not simply remembering the past. It is an active, courageous return to the places within you that still echo with unspoken truths.

It is the first and most essential phase of the Self-Empowerment Breakthrough Process™. For many, it is the one most resisted; not because it lacks power—but because it holds too much pain.

But here's what I want you to remember: Before you became who the world said you are, you were divinely programmed to be your True Self. Reflection provides an opportunity for you to return home to that sacred person and that sacred space.

Pause & Reflect: What parts of yourself feel most authentic—and which feel borrowed from someone else's expectations?

What Reflection Really Is

Reflection is the conscious act of witnessing your thoughts, beliefs, emotional responses, and past experiences through the lens of awareness—not judgment. It is the moment you stop being the story and become the storyteller. It is not rumination. It is revelation.

From a neuroscientific perspective, reflection activates the prefrontal cortex, the part of the brain responsible for insight, emotional regulation, and executive decision-making. This activation increases our ability to observe patterns, interrupt emotional reactivity, and access higher cognitive functioning.

From a spiritual perspective, reflection is sacred. In Eastern mindfulness traditions, it is considered the doorway to liberation. In

New Thought philosophy, reflection is how the soul becomes aware of its own entanglements so that it may return to alignment with its divine nature. Joel Goldsmith, author of *The Infinite Way*, called it "the silence in which Truth is revealed."

When you reflect with intention, you create space between stimulus and response, between memory and meaning. In that space, healing begins.

A Broader Story: The Unspoken Wounds That Shape Us

Take the story of Lena—an accomplished entrepreneur running a thriving six-figure business. She was known for her brilliance, her precision, and her tireless work ethic. But Lena had a habit she couldn't shake: she never let herself pause. She feared stillness. She worked through illness, avoided vacations, and called herself "productive" when in truth, she was avoiding something deeper.

During a private coaching session, she finally allowed herself to reflect and what surfaced shocked her. At age nine, Lena's mother had fallen into a deep depression. As the eldest child, Lena stepped in. She cooked, cleaned, and made straight A's—not for approval, but to keep the house from collapsing.

She had become the rescuer. The achiever. The invisible need-bearer.
Now, at 42, she was still that child in disguise.

Reflection didn't fix Lena, but it gave her the first honest glimpse of the story she'd been unconsciously reliving for years.

The Purpose of Reflecting on Old Patterns

There is a reason we don't always see our patterns. The subconscious mind operates like a film reel on loop—running below the level of conscious awareness. Unless we stop to examine the script, we assume the movie is real.

Reflection gives us a way to:

- Recognize the core beliefs that were formed in pain or protection.
- See how those beliefs shaped our behaviors, relationships, and self-concept.
- Gently question the validity of the stories we've mistaken for truth.

Reflection is not about blame. It is about clarity. And clarity is power.

Pause & Reflect: Can you name one belief or habit that you now recognize as a pattern rather than a permanent truth?

Courageous Reflection vs. Self-Judgment

Healing reflection is not the same as negative self-judgment. It does not sound like:

- *"Why can't I get it right?"*
- *"What's wrong with me?"*
- *"I should've known better."*

That's not reflection. That's self-punishment.

True reflection sounds like:

- *"What do I believe right now?"*
- *"Where did that belief come from?"*
- *"Is this thought mine—or someone else's?"*
- *"How is this belief serving me—or limiting me?"*

This approach is grounded in metacognition—a scientific term that refers to thinking about one's thinking. Research shows that developing metacognitive awareness strengthens emotional intelligence, increases self-regulation, and supports long-term mental well-being.

This Is the Chapter Where You Begin to Identify Your Core Values and Non-Negotiable Beliefs

Reflection is where you first uncover the hidden architecture of your self-concept. This is where you discover not only what you believe—but why you believe it.

Here is where you'll begin to ask:

- *What beliefs did I inherit that I never chose?*
- *What do I say I believe, but live as if I don't?*
- *What are my core values and do I live them?*
- *What values do I hold that I've never fully claimed?*

This is where you identify and claim your non-negotiables—the principles, truths, and soul-codes that anchor your most authentic life. But you can't claim them until you confront the ones you've unconsciously adopted and lived by.

Pause & Reflect: Take a few minutes and reflect on these questions. Journal about the ones that speak to you.

Why Reflection Matters for Mind Mastery

Mind mastery is impossible without self-awareness. Here's why:

You can't rewire what you can't name.
If a belief lives in the shadows, it cannot be consciously challenged. Awareness is the precondition for all neurological rewiring. Neuroplasticity confirms that new neural pathways form in direct response to focused attention, intention, and emotional engagement.

You can't reclaim your power while avoiding your pain.
The parts of you that you've disowned—because they felt shameful, unworthy, or weak—are often the very places where your true power is hiding. To reflect is to remember the whole of who you are, including your shadow self—not just the polished version.

You can't embody your divine identity while clinging to inherited limitations.
In metaphysical terms, your consciousness is a creative force. If your mind is saturated with untrue beliefs, your life will reflect them—even if your soul longs for something more. In other words, reflection clears the debris so your essence can shine through.

Pause & Reflect: Where in your life do you feel the gap between who you've been taught to be and who you sense you truly are?

What Makes This Process Sacred

In nearly every spiritual tradition, self-examination is a precursor to enlightenment.
In Buddhism, it is *vipassana*—insight into the nature of reality.
In Christianity, it is repentance—not guilt, but a radical turning of the mind.
In Kabbalah, it is *hitbonenut*—deep contemplation.
In metaphysics, it is the mirror in which the soul returns to its original image.

Reflection is not about fixing.
It is about freeing.

Reflection in Action: An Integrative Practice

To begin this phase of your journey, set aside 20 minutes each day for the next week.
Use a journal or voice recorder and ask yourself:

- What have I been pretending not to know?
- What old story do I keep retelling—and why?
- What emotions am I avoiding by staying busy?
- What role have I adopted to feel safe?
- What would I have to let go of to be fully free?

Let your answers surprise you. Let them shake you. Let them soften you.

You're not trying to be right. You're trying to be real.

Conclusion: It's Time To Remember Who You Are

You do not need to be perfect to be powerful.

You only need to be present—with yourself, with your story, with your truth.

This is how mastery begins: not in control, but in clarity.

In the next chapter, we'll explore what comes after seeing the pattern. We move into *Reimagining*—the sacred practice of envisioning a new self, a new story, and a new future beyond your conditioning.

But for now, I encourage you to just sit with this.

Look in the mirror.

And begin to remember who you were before the world told you who you should be.

Awareness opens the door,

reflection walks you through it,

and in that sacred crossing, your soul remembers what your mind forgot—

that every moment of reflection is a quiet rebirth,

and every act of seeing yourself clearly is an act of power.

Deep Dive Practice: Remembering Who You Are

1. What patterns keep showing up in my life, no matter how much I try to change the external?
2. Whose approval am I still unconsciously seeking?

3. When did I first learn that love had to be earned, or that I wasn't enough as I am?
4. What memories still carry emotional charge—and what belief did I form in that moment?
5. What truth am I finally ready to claim?

"When you are brave enough to face what is, you make space for what can be. Your power doesn't come from perfection—it comes from being present with yourself."
                                        ~Dr. Sue Carter Collins

---

Chapter 9

Phase 2: Reimagining – Creating a New Vision of Your Empowered Self

"Before you can become her, you must first
be willing to see her.
The woman within you who already exists—
whole, wise, and waiting for your yes."

~Dr. Sue Carter Collins

Don't Be Afraid to Dream

If reflection is the mirror, reimagining is the window.
Reflection reveals what has been.

Reimagining opens you to what could be.

It is the practice of envisioning a life beyond your current conditioning—of choosing, with intention, who you are becoming and how you wish to live.

Reimagining is the second phase of the Self-Empowerment Breakthrough (SEB) Process™. It is the bridge between self-awareness and self-authorship. It asks not, *"What happened to me?"* but rather, *"What is now possible because of me?"*

This is where your inner reality begins to shift. Not because your circumstances have changed—but because you have.

In this chapter, you're being asked to assume a child-like attitude of curiosity and wonder. Open the floodgates of your imagination. Don't be afraid to dream.

Dream Big!

The Power of Imagination: A Multidimensional Tool for Change

For centuries, imagination was dismissed as fanciful or naive. Today, science, spirituality, and psychology all confirm what mystics have always known: imagination is not passive. It is creative, directive, and transformative.

Neuroscience shows that the brain does not distinguish between real and vividly imagined experiences. Harvard psychologist Daniel Schacter discovered that the same neural pathways used to recall memories are also activated when we imagine the future. This process allows us to mentally simulate outcomes and emotionally rehearse new possibilities.

Dr. Joe Dispenza, in *Breaking the Habit of Being Yourself*, adds that when visualization is paired with elevated emotions like joy or gratitude, the body begins to chemically experience that vision as reality.

Cell biologist Bruce Lipton explains that beliefs—conscious or unconscious—directly influence the chemical environment of our cells. When you hold a vision of yourself as whole, capable, or worthy, you are literally altering your biology to support that version of you.

From the field of heart-brain science, Gregg Braden's research shows that when your heart and brain are in vibrational alignment, your electromagnetic signal is amplified. This coherence affects your nervous system, your emotional state, and your ability to manifest outcomes.

From a metaphysical standpoint, vision is not fantasy—it is conscious creation. Neville Goddard taught: *"Assume the feeling of the wish fulfilled."* When you vividly imagine and emotionally accept a new reality, it is impressed upon your subconscious and echoed into the unseen realm.

Pause & Reflect

- When was the last time you allowed yourself to imagine without limits?
- What feelings come up when you think about dreaming bigger—excitement, fear, resistance?

Spiritual Vision Is Not Goal-Setting

In New Thought and metaphysical circles, vision is not about egoic ambition—it is a sacred remembering of who your soul already knows you are.

Michael Bernard Beckwith teaches that true vision is not something you create—it is something you tune into. You ask, *"What is seeking to emerge through me?"* and *"Who must I become to allow it?"*

Reimagining is not just about possibility—it is about permission. It is about revoking the old agreements that said you weren't enough, that you should play small, that your dreams were foolish.

Instead, you say yes to new agreements. Agreements based in soul, sovereignty, and truth. Agreements you consciously choose.

The Emotional Resistance to Vision

Although reimagining sounds beautiful, many people avoid it because it requires believing in what isn't yet visible. It activates fears of disappointment, failure, or unworthiness. It asks you to dream again—after years of being told to "be realistic."

Reimagining demands that you be vulnerable. That you risk hope, that you risk faith.

Thich Nhat Hanh reminds us: *"You don't have to wait until all suffering is gone to be happy."* Similarly, you don't have to wait until all fear is gone to have a vision. Your vision can rise alongside your healing.

Pause & Reflect

- What excuses or fears come up when you try to imagine your best self?
- Who told you it was unsafe to dream—and do you still want to carry that belief?

Sandi's Story: The Woman She Almost Forgot

During a coaching session, Sandi, a brilliant woman in her early 40s, broke down in tears.

"I don't know who I am anymore," she whispered. "I know what I've survived. I know how to work. But I have no idea what I want."

She had built a successful business, raised two children, and survived a decade-long emotionally abusive marriage. She was tired of surviving—but terrified of imagining something more.

I asked her, "If you were free from all that…if you could have anything you wanted…if you could be anyone you wanted to be… who would you be?"

She closed her eyes and saw a woman in a red dress, speaking on a stage, powerful and unapologetic. That vision wasn't fantasy. It was a memory from the future. That woman was already within her—just waiting to be released.

How to Reimagine with Power and Precision

Reimagining is not an abstract exercise. It is mental rehearsal and energetic alignment. Here's a process to help you get started.

1. **Enter Sacred Space.** Light a candle. Breathe deeply. Invite your higher self forward.
2. **Ask Your Soul.** Who am I becoming?
3. **Feel It Fully.** What do you see, hear, and feel in this new life?
4. **Document It.** Journal it. Speak it. Paint it. Give it form.
5. **Anchor the Identity.** Use affirmations rooted in truth:
    o *"I am safe to expand."*
    o *"I am worthy of joy."*
    o *"I am already becoming."*

Remember, you are not inventing a new self. You are reconnecting with the original one.

Why This Matters for Mind Mastery

The brain defaults to the familiar. If you don't provide it with a new vision, it will return to old scripts—even painful ones—because they are known.

Mind mastery is not only about breaking patterns—it is about replacing them with empowered blueprints. When your vision is clear, your choices align. When your vision is felt, your nervous system begins to believe. When your vision is repeated, your brain rewires.

This is not wishful thinking.
This is neuroplasticity.
This is epigenetics.
This is metaphysical creation.

And this is why vision matters.

Conclusion: Say Yes to the Vision and Release What No Longer Fits

Many of us are afraid to dream because we don't know what the future holds. Although we may want answers in advance, the truth is that there are some things we will never know—and that's okay. This is when you turn inward and lean on your faith.

Accept that you don't have to know exactly how your vision will come to life. You don't have to map every step, predict every turn, or prove your worthiness to receive it.

You just have to say yes.
Yes to the self you're becoming.
Yes to the life that's already reaching for you.
Yes to the power that rises when you choose to believe in something beautiful.

Because vision isn't about knowing the how.
It's about trusting the who—
And that who is you.

Yet even as this new vision expands, traces of the old story may rise to meet it. The mind, the body, and the heart remember what was, even as the soul reaches for what can be. This is not regression—it's invitation.

The next stage of your journey is not about dreaming more—it's about **releasing** what no longer fits inside the dream.

Awareness awakens the path.
Vision lights the way.
But release clears the space so transformation can take place.

Deep Dive Practice: Becoming HER

1. What version of yourself are you most longing to become—and what beliefs or roles must you release to make space for her?
2. If nothing from your past defined you, who would you be free to be right now?
3. What does your reimagined life look, feel, and sound like?
4. Where have you been living from survival instead of vision? What would shift if you led from possibility?
5. What one belief, if fully embraced, would radically change how you show up in the world?

"You are not waiting on a miracle. You are the miracle—activated by vision, aligned by choice, and made real through your belief."
~Dr. Sue Carter Collins

Chapter 10

Phase 3: Releasing – Letting Go of the Old Stories

*"You cannot become who you were born to
be while still making excuses
for who you had to be to survive."*

~Dr. Sue Carter Collins

When the Vision Becomes Clear —but the Past Still Lingers

Every vision calls forth its counterpart—the memories, emotions, and energies that must be released for the new self to emerge. Once you say yes to your becoming, everything within you that was built for survival begins to stir. The nervous system remembers. The mind questions. The heart hesitates between the comfort of the old and the pull of the new.

You can see the woman you are becoming.
You can feel the possibility of that life.
But your body still carries memories.

Your mind still loops on old scripts.
Your nervous system still flinches with the residue of who you used to be.

This is the threshold of transformation.
It is not punishment. It is purification.
It is the space between your vision and your reality—
the transformation gap.

The liminal space.
The space where life is still happening.

To cross it, you must learn to release.

When you stand at this threshold, everything in you will want to reach back for what is familiar—even when that familiarity has caused your suffering. Releasing asks you to do the opposite: to let go of the past and trust that the unknown will hold you. It is not a denial of what was. It is a declaration that what was can no longer define what will be.

Why Releasing Matters

Reflection reveals the patterns. Reimagining births the vision.
But releasing is what makes room for that vision to live.

You cannot pour new wine into an old vessel, nor sustain a new life while clinging to the energy of the old one. Releasing is both science and spirit—part neurological rewiring, part soul liberation. It is the alchemy through which you shed the weight of what no longer serves your expansion and return the energy once trapped in survival back to creation.

Releasing is not simply about letting go of memories; it is the sacred dissolving of old imprints that constrain your mind, body, and spirit. It's about freeing yourself of:

- The self-concepts that no longer serve you
- The protective identities you no longer need
- The trauma-bound loyalties you no longer wish to carry
- The nervous system responses that once ensured survival but now sabotage

Some of the most common expressions that arise in the Release phase include:

- Old narratives: "I'm not enough." "People always leave."
- Inherited beliefs: "Success must be hard." "If I shine, I'll be punished."
- Embodied fear: Nervous system overactivation, hypervigilance, people-pleasing
- Shame stories: About your body, your past, your voice, or your worth
- Energetic contracts: Agreements to stay small, silent, or invisible to keep others comfortable

Releasing is not a one-time occurrence. It spirals—like a slinky stretched across time. You may release a belief at one level and revisit it again later, meeting it from a new vantage point, with deeper awareness and more compassion. Each return is not regression—it is refinement, a sacred return to yourself at higher levels of clarity and power.

So, releasing is not about blaming.
It is about reclaiming.

Pause & Reflect

- Where in my life am I still holding onto an old identity that no longer reflects who I am?
- Do I see my return to familiar patterns as failure— or as an invitation to meet myself with deeper compassion?

Maya's Story: The Grief Beneath the Armor

Maya, a high-achieving executive, came to a coaching session convinced she had a clarity issue. She wanted help "thinking through her next move." What emerged, though, wasn't strategy— it was sorrow.

Beneath her polished language and leadership tone was a woman holding decades of tension in her chest. During one somatic exercise, her body began to shake, tears welled in her eyes, and then a single sentence escaped her lips:

"I've been carrying my mother's pain my whole life."

The words stunned even her. What followed was not a breakdown, but a breakthrough—a release. Years of suppressed grief rose to the surface. Not all at once. Not violently. But honestly.

Releasing didn't make Maya less capable. It made her more whole. And from that wholeness, she finally gained clarity.

The Science and Soul of Letting Go

Dr. Bessel van der Kolk, author of *The Body Keeps the Score*, reminds us that trauma is not just remembered in the mind—it is stored in the body. To truly release an old pattern, you must engage the whole system: mental, emotional, energetic, and physical.

Every time you replay a thought, you reinforce a neural circuit. But when you interrupt that circuit and choose differently, you prune old connections and make space for new ones to form. This is the gift of neuroplasticity: the brain is not fixed—and neither are you.

Dr. Caroline Leaf teaches that deliberate thought rewiring requires not just awareness, but replacement. You don't just stop a thought; you install a new one. You don't just release a feeling; you retrain your nervous system to respond differently. You don't just let go of an old identity—you honor it, thank it for its service, and consciously choose to evolve beyond it.

Energetic Releasing and Soul Fragmentation

Louise Hay and Caroline Myss remind us that releasing isn't just emotional—it's vibrational. It involves reclaiming the parts of yourself that fragmented in moments of fear, shame, betrayal, or trauma.

- **Louise Hay**, in *You Can Heal Your Life*, emphasized that every dis-ease or chronic condition corresponds to emotional patterning. Her affirmations were not mere positive thinking—they were energetic corrections that reprogram the subconscious and open the way for release.

- **Caroline Myss**, in *Anatomy of the Spirit*, showed how trauma, betrayal, or self-abandonment create disruptions in the chakra system and "sacred contracts." *"Your biography becomes your biology,"* she wrote. Releasing is the act of naming the wound, reclaiming the energy lost to it, and calling your power back.

This mirrors what depth psychology calls **soul fragmentation**: when parts of your consciousness dissociate in moments of overwhelm. Releasing is the process of reintegration—of bringing those parts home.

Pause & Reflect: Integrating the Layers of Healing

Before diving into the science of release, take a breath and notice what this chapter has already stirred within you. Healing unfolds across multiple dimensions—emotional, physical, energetic, and spiritual—and each carries its own wisdom and language.

Ask yourself:

- *Which layer of healing feels most alive for me right now—emotional, physical, or spiritual?*
- *What am I ready to let rise to the surface for understanding or release, even if I don't yet have words for it?*
- *Where might I still be holding on—not out of resistance, but out of fear of who I'll be without the old story?*

Let these questions rest gently in your awareness. You're not analyzing—you're allowing. Healing deepens when you stop trying to fix what you think is broken and start listening to what's ready to be free.

Science and spirit are about to meet on the same ground—the body, the mind, and the nervous system. As you read on, remember: every theory you'll encounter here confirms what your soul already knows.

Scientific Support: Trauma, Memory, and Integration

Modern psychology echoes these truths and gives language to what the soul has always known: the mind and body are partners in healing. What metaphysical teachers describe as fragmentation, science recognizes as the body's adaptive response to overwhelm. Together, they affirm that the path to freedom involves not just understanding the mind, but reintegrating the self at every level—mental, emotional, physical, and spiritual.

- **Dissociation – The Mind's Emergency Exit**

Dissociation is the mind's emergency exit. It allows you to detach from unbearable pain so you can survive the moment—but when it persists, it divides you from your own experience. This psychological separation protects you during crisis but can later create emotional numbness, memory gaps, or a sense of disconnection from self and others. Healing involves gently inviting awareness back into the body and allowing the mind and emotions to safely reconnect.

- **Implicit Memory – The Body Remembers What the Mind Forgets**

Even when conscious recall fades, the body remembers. Dr. Bessel van der Kolk's research on trauma demonstrates that experiences stored as *implicit memory*—the sensory and emotional imprints of past pain—continue to shape behavior until they are consciously released. Muscles tense, breathing shortens, and emotions repeat until they are acknowledged and integrated. Somatic and mindfulness-based practices help transform these memories from survival responses into self-awareness, restoring harmony between body and mind.

- **Neuroception – The Body's Constant Scan for Safety (Dr. Stephen Porges)**

According to Dr. Stephen Porges, creator of Polyvagal Theory, the body constantly scans for cues of safety or threat—a subconscious process called *neuroception*. After trauma, this system can become hypervigilant, interpreting neutral experiences as dangerous and keeping the nervous system in a chronic state of defense. Restoring calm through breathwork, grounding, and supportive relationships retrains the nervous system to recognize safety again, allowing energy to flow freely.

- **Integration – The Return to Wholeness (Dr. Dan Siegel)**

Dr. Dan Siegel describes mental health as "integration across the system." Trauma, he explains, creates *dis-integration*—a loss of connection between the different parts of the brain and self. Healing occurs as those connections are restored and the emotional, cognitive, and bodily aspects of experience begin to work together again. As Siegel notes, "Where there is trauma, there is dis-integration. Healing is the return to wholeness." Integration doesn't erase the past; it reorganizes it so that memory no longer governs the present.

Science and spirit converge here: release is essential for integration, healing, and transformation. Letting go of stored pain, outdated neural patterns, and protective identities is both a psychological and spiritual act. As you soften into safety and surrender what no longer serves you, your mind, body, and soul realign in harmony. What once felt fragmented becomes the architecture of wisdom—proof that wholeness was never lost, only waiting to be remembered.

A Personal Story: What I Had to Release to Rise

When I first envisioned the life I wanted—the woman on the stage, flowing in her power—I thought I just needed to visualize harder.

But belief alone wasn't enough. My body still clenched at old memories. My voice still trembled when I spoke my truth. My mind still shut down when I reached for more.

I realized I had to release more than circumstances. I had to release the version of myself who had learned only to survive.

The girl who thought she was stupid because a teacher said she couldn't write.
The girl who thought she was worthless because a doctor violated her.
The woman who believed her worth depended on her degrees, her performance, her perfection.

I had to feel the grief. The rage. The fear.
I had to tell the truth about what I had survived.
And then—bit by bit—I had to let her go.

Not reject her.
But honor her.
Thank her.
Release her.
So I could rise.

How to Release What No Longer Serves You

Although there is no one-size-fits-all formula for release, the following sacred practice integrates both psychology and spirit. Each step is an act of remembrance—helping you let go of what no longer aligns with your becoming and return to the truth of who you are.

1. **Name the Story**

   Bring it into the light. Write, speak, or simply acknowledge the belief or memory that still shapes how you see yourself. Ask, "*When did I first start believing this—and what was I trying to protect?*" Naming it loosens its power and begins the energetic unraveling.

2. **Feel It to Free It**

   Suppressed emotion is stored energy. Give yourself permission to grieve, rage, cry, tremble, or simply breathe through it.

   Healing happens through embodiment, not avoidance. Emotion is *energy in motion*—let it move so it can leave.

3. **Interrupt the Loop**

   Notice the moment you start replaying the old story. Pause. Breathe. Choose a new thought, even if it feels unfamiliar.

   This is the practical application of neuroplasticity: every interruption weakens the old wiring and strengthens the new.

4. **Use the Body**

   The body is your ally in release. Engage in movement, breathwork, stretching, or tapping (EFT) to move stuck energy through your system.

Remember, the nervous system learns safety through experience, not theory. Let your body teach your mind that you are safe to let go.

5. **Invoke the Divine**

   Release is not a solo act. Invite Spirit, Source, or your Higher Self to help carry what feels too heavy.

   Prayer, meditation, or surrender statements such as *"I am willing to release this with grace"* open the energetic channel for transformation.

6. **Write a Release Statement**

   Seal the process with conscious declaration. Write in the present tense, as if it is already done:

   "I release the belief that I must earn love through perfection. I bless it, thank it, and set it free. I choose truth, peace, and freedom."

   Speak it aloud. Burn or safely dispose of the paper as a symbolic act of closure.

Release is not a single moment—it is a practice of devotion. Each time you consciously let go, you strengthen the frequency of freedom. You teach your mind, body, and soul that it is safe to live unburdened. Over time, this becomes not an event, but a way of being.

Conclusion: The Power of Sacred Release

Mind mastery is not about control—it's about making conscious choices.

Releasing is the sacred act of returning what no longer belongs to your becoming. Each time you let go of an old identity, belief, or story, you reclaim a fragment of your power and redirect your energy toward expansion.

You cannot choose a new path while dragging the weight of the old one behind you. Nor can you live in the past, present, and future simultaneously. Before you can thrive, you must surrender the thoughts, beliefs, and behaviors that are holding you down—keeping you bound to a version of yourself that no longer exists.

To release is to choose trust over tension, faith over familiarity, and alignment over attachment.
This is where the alchemy happens—where grief becomes grace, endings become openings, and letting go becomes liberation.

In the next chapter, we move into Reprogramming—the phase where you consciously rewrite your mental codes and install new patterns that reflect your truth. Because once you've cleared the space, your soul is ready for new architecture—one built from intention, not inheritance.

Release empties your hands. Reprogramming teaches you how to build again.

Deep Dive Practice: Are You Willing to Let Go?

1. What belief, pattern, or identity are you most ready to release—and what new freedom would that open for you?
2. Where in your life are you still entangled in the past, and how is it showing up today?
3. What part of you is waiting to be honored and set free?

4. Which memory still carries emotional charge—and how could releasing it change your story?
5. What are you finally ready to forgive, not for others, but for your own freedom?

"Release is not the end of a story. It is the beginning of a sacred pause where the soul exhales and makes room for what's next."

~Dr. Sue Carter Collins

Chapter 11

Phase 4: Reprogramming – Installing the Inner Architecture of Empowerment

From Theory to Committed Action

There comes a moment in every transformation when insight alone is no longer enough.

You can reflect on your patterns. You can reimagine a new life. You can release what no longer serves you. But unless you install new ways of thinking, feeling, and behaving, the old wiring will keep rerouting you back to the past—a past you must transcend in order to embody the new you.

This is the essence of reprogramming. It is the fourth phase of the Self-Empowerment Breakthrough Process™—and it is foundational. Reprogramming is where your new identity is installed, rehearsed, and reinforced through consistent, conscious alignment.
It is where mind mastery moves from theory to committed action.
From thoughts to transformation.
From ideas to manifestation.

Why Reprogramming Is Essential

Your mind is an amazing thing. Despite all that it does to keep you alive, its default setting is not expansion but familiarity. That means no matter how much you reflect, release, or reimagine, if your subconscious beliefs are still wired for fear, scarcity, shame, or self-doubt, they will override your conscious desires.

Dr. Bruce Lipton, cell biologist and author of *The Biology of Belief*, explains that the subconscious mind controls 95% of your thoughts, behaviors, and emotional responses. Unless it is intentionally rewired, it will continue running the same outdated programs that were installed during childhood or trauma. What this means is clear:

"You can repeat affirmations all day, but if your subconscious believes the opposite, it will win every time."

So, if you consciously believe that you deserve love, success, or visibility—but your subconscious associates those things with rejection, punishment, or loss—you will unconsciously sabotage the very things you say you want. That is why reprogramming is not optional. It is essential—this is where neuroplasticity comes in.

Pause & Reflect: Where do you notice your subconscious overriding your conscious goals? Think of a moment when you wanted to expand—but found yourself shrinking instead. What belief might be running that script?

Neuroplasticity – The Brain's Ability to Change

Neuroplasticity is the brain's lifelong capacity to form new neural pathways. Every time you think a thought or perform a behavior, you strengthen a neural network. When you repeat that thought or behavior consistently, it becomes a default pathway—what we call a habit or belief.

Dr. Joe Dispenza, author of *Breaking the Habit of Being Yourself*, teaches:

"Neurons that fire together, wire together."

This is known as the Hebbian principle.
Unused circuits are pruned away by the brain to conserve energy. Emotionally intense thoughts, especially traumatic ones, strengthen circuits faster. This explains why painful beliefs feel so deeply embedded—and why emotionally energized affirmations and intentional rewiring can expedite change.

Dr. Dispenza also teaches: "You cannot create a new reality from the same personality. You must become someone new."
So reprogramming is about firing new thoughts, feelings, and actions in alignment with who you're becoming.

Habit Formation: The Real Timeline

When we speak of transformation and behavior modification, it is necessary first to address the myth that a new habit can be formed in just 21 days.

A study from University College London led by Dr. Phillippa Lally (2010) concluded that it takes, on average, 66 days for a new behavior to become automatic. However, considering the uniqueness of individuals and their environments, the actual time spanned from 18 to 254 days. The more emotionally ingrained the habit—especially those linked to trauma—the longer reprogramming tends to take.

Dr. Wendy Wood, author of *Good Habits, Bad Habits*, stated:

"Habits don't change just because we want them to. They change because we repeatedly perform the new behavior in consistent contexts until it becomes the brain's default."

Pause & Reflect: The Practice of Repetition

1. Think of a time when you tried to change a belief or behavior but found yourself slipping back into old patterns. What emotions surfaced—frustration, shame, discouragement, or doubt? What might those feelings reveal about the deeper belief still running the show?
2. What new behavior, if practiced with patience and intention, could begin to reshape both your neural wiring and your sense of self?

As you reflect, remember that repetition is more than a mental exercise—it's an energetic declaration. Each time you practice a new thought or behavior, you're not just rewiring your brain; you're realigning your vibration with a higher possibility. This is where science and soul converge—the moment when neuroplasticity becomes metaphysical creation.

The Metaphysics of Mind Repatterning

Metaphysically, reprogramming is the art of consciously directing thought into form.

New Thought leader Neville Goddard taught that the subconscious mind is the creative medium through which reality is manifested. He believed:

"The subconscious does not argue. It accepts whatever the conscious mind impresses upon it."

Spiritual teacher Florence Scovel Shinn echoed this truth. She taught:

"Change your thoughts, and in the twinkling of an eye, all your conditions change."

So reprogramming impresses upon the individual a new energetic blueprint.

The more often you resort to it—through thought, feeling, and embodiment—the faster it becomes your default vibration.

In other words: thought becomes belief, belief becomes behavior, behavior becomes identity.

A Personal Story: My Rewiring Moment

When I began reprogramming my mind, it wasn't elegant. It was awkward and uncomfortable. Every empowering affirmation I spoke felt like a lie. I felt so dishonest.
But I kept going.

I wrote new beliefs on sticky notes and taped them on mirrors and walls throughout the house. I wanted to always have them in my line of sight.
I spoke life over myself when my inner critic tried to replay old shame.
I practiced emotional self-regulation when I wanted to shut down or spiral.

I interrupted the pattern with thoughts like: "I see you." "Change the narrative." "Stay focused."
I encouraged myself by saying: "You can do this." "Know your value and your worth." "Never compromise, never settle, never regret, and never give up."

I reminded myself: "You have a choice." "You're the CEO of your life. Stand in your power."
I resonated with my soul which called out to me: "Master your mind." "Interrupt your thinking." "Reframe your thoughts."

It didn't happen fast. But over time, something shifted.

One day I recognized that the disempowering thoughts were fewer and slower in coming.
I embraced my new persona.
I stopped waiting to feel confident.

I started acting from confidence—until my nervous system caught up.

In the end I realized reprogramming didn't change me into someone else.
It returned me to who I was before the world told me who I wasn't.

Pause & Reflect: What daily practices could you use to rewire your own thinking? What reminders or affirmations could you place in your environment to keep you aligned with the person you're becoming?

A Client Story: Terri's Inner Reset

Terri was a high-powered executive who looked confident on the outside—but every major opportunity triggered deep anxiety and self-sabotage. In our weekly coaching sessions, she discovered that her subconscious held the belief: *If I stand out, they won't like me.*

That belief had originated in middle school, when she was bullied after winning an academic award. Using a synergistic combination of visualization, energy healing, and somatic breathwork, we were able to release the emotional charge associated with Terri's memory. We then anchored a new belief: *It's safe to shine. I am protected and powerful.*

Three months later, Terri delivered a keynote speech at a national conference. When I asked how she felt afterward, she said, "I didn't feel nervous. I felt like I belonged."

Tools and Modalities That Support Reprogramming

While daily affirmations and mirror work are powerful tools, they are even more effective when synergistically integrated with other modalities. Here are a few commonly used methods:

- **EFT (Emotional Freedom Technique):** Uses tapping on acupressure points to calm the nervous system and reduce emotional intensity, making new beliefs easier to install.
- **Guided Visualization:** Engages the imagination and emotion to rehearse new outcomes and impress them into the subconscious mind.
- **Hypnotherapy:** Bypasses the critical mind to directly access and rewire subconscious beliefs.
- **Neuro-Linguistic Programming (NLP):** Helps reframe internal dialogue and anchor empowering states using language and behavior modeling.
- **Somatic Practices:** Involves breathwork, movement, and body awareness to integrate new beliefs at the cellular level.
- **Spiritual Alignment Practices:** Includes prayer, meditation, and affirmation aligned with Universal Law. These practices build energetic coherence between intention and manifestation.

No one method will work for everyone. Readers are encouraged to choose the tools that resonate most deeply.

Conclusion: Reprogramming as Embodied Power

As we prepare to transition into the final stage of the SEB Process™, remember that mind mastery is not about controlling every thought—

it's about training your inner world to match your highest truth. You are not a victim of your past programming; you are the architect of your future design.

Reprogramming is where faith meets repetition, and commitment meets action.
It's how you collapse the gap between who you were and who you are becoming.
It's how you embody HER—and create the life you were always meant to live.

In the next chapter, we'll move from reprogramming to embodiment—the phase where change no longer requires effort, because it has become identity. This is where the new wiring integrates fully into your being and transformation becomes your natural way of life.

Because true mastery isn't just what you think—it's what you live.

Deep Dive Practice: Begin Your Inner Rewiring

1. What belief are you most ready to rewrite—and why now?
2. Where in your life do you still default to old scripts even when you know better?
3. What emotion or memory do you need to release to anchor your new belief?
4. What daily ritual can help you reinforce your new identity until it becomes your natural state?
5. How can your spiritual practices support your rewiring and integration?

"The mind replays what it knows. But with intention and repetition, you can teach it something new. You can teach it what is possible."
~Dr. Sue Carter Collins

Chapter 12

Phase 5: Recreating – Becoming the Embodied Expression of Your Reimagined Life

"Embodiment is the final initiation—where wisdom becomes walk, and alignment becomes the way you live."

~Dr. Sue Carter Collins

Healing Is Not the End

It is the beginning of who you now have the capacity to become.

When you reach the recreation phase, you have done some deep work. You've reflected on the past, reimagined your future, released what no longer serves you, and reprogrammed your mind with new beliefs. However, until you live from those beliefs—until they become not just what you know, but who you are—the transformation remains mainly theoretical.

Recreating is about actual embodiment.

It is the culmination of your inner work becoming your outer reality. It is where empowered thinking becomes empowered being.

As Dr. Wayne Dyer wrote, "You'll see it when you believe it." This is the inverse of the common cultural phrase—and it gets to the heart of Phase 5.
When your internal state changes, your external life cannot remain the same.

Pause & Reflect: Where have you already begun to see your inner transformation reflected in your external world? What evidence—large or small—tells you that something within you has shifted?

Why Recreation Matters

Every transformation requires integration. It's not enough to feel better or think differently in isolated moments. Your identity must evolve. Your habits must reflect your highest self. Your nervous system must internalize safety, power, and alignment.

This is the final phase of the SEB Process because it provides evidence that your healing transformation is underway.

Dr. Dan Siegel, Professor of Psychiatry and co-director of the Mindfulness Awareness Research Center, describes mental health as "integration across the system." The healed mind is one where thought, feeling, behavior, and purpose align. Recreation is that alignment in motion.

Neville Goddard described it this way: "To be transformed, the whole basis of your thoughts must change. But your thoughts cannot change unless you have new ideas, for you think from your ideas." Thus, to embody the life you've envisioned, you must consistently act from it—not toward it.

The Psychology of Identity Reinforcement

Recreating your life requires reinforcing a new identity across time, space, and behavior. Psychologist James Clear, in his work on identity-based habits, asserts that "every action you take is a vote for the person you want to become." Habits are not merely behavior—they are expressions of who you believe yourself to be.

If you want to become someone who honors her voice, you must speak up—even when your hands shake and your voice trembles. If you want to live as someone who trusts herself, you must make decisions—even when fear whispers otherwise.

This consistent, embodied repetition is what makes your new self-concept stick. The brain consolidates identity through enactment, not intention alone.

In his study on the neuroscience of self-concept, Dr. David Creswell found that identity becomes more neurologically stable when it is linked to repeated actions and emotional investment. This means we become who we practice being.

The Energetics of Embodied Living

Living from your future self is an energetic act.

According to metaphysical teachers such as Joel Goldsmith and Dr. Sue Morter, your vibrational frequency—the energetic signature you emit—shapes what you attract and sustain.

Goldsmith noted, "There is no power external to you. All power is within, and must be realized there before it can manifest outwardly."

Dr. Sue Morter, in *The Energy Codes*, teaches that embodiment means shifting from "thinking" your transformation to "being" your transformation. When energy moves through the body with coherence, your presence becomes your power.

Thus, to recreate your life, you must first become a vibrational match to the life you claim. Recreation isn't just about affirming the new you—it's about living from her.

A Personal Story: The Shift Into Sovereignty

When I stepped into full alignment with the woman I was becoming, it wasn't because everything outside of me changed. It was because I changed how I showed up within it.

After decades of work—degrees, healing, achievements—there came a moment when I looked in the mirror and didn't just see my past. I saw my presence.

I stopped apologizing for my voice. I stopped editing my truth. I stopped proving, performing, and pleasing.

I started speaking from my inner wisdom—even when others didn't understand it.

I started dressing for the future me—not for the approval of others.

I started holding boundaries, not out of anger, but out of deep self-respect.

I stopped asking for permission and started being my authentic self. That's when my life began to shift. Not perfectly, but unmistakably.

That's when I realized I wasn't just thinking new thoughts—I was living them.

Pause & Reflect: When was the last time you caught a glimpse of your "future self" showing up through you—whether in your confidence, your words, or your presence? How did it feel to meet her?

A Story from Practice: Claiming the Role of Visionary

One of my clients, named Alana, came to me feeling stuck. She had done years of therapy, completed a coaching certification program, and even launched a business—but still found herself shrinking in rooms that required her leadership.

As we worked through the healing process, she uncovered a childhood belief that she would be disliked for outshining others. She successfully reprogrammed that belief with the truth: "I am here to shine. My light liberates others. I am walking in my purpose."

But the real shift didn't come until she actually walked into a boardroom, sat at the head of the table, and began speaking with authority. Yes, she was nervous. Her hands shook and her voice cracked, but she kept going.

That act was the turning point for her.

She knew she had crossed the line from preparation into embodiment.

She was no longer waiting to become a leader.

She had arrived.

A Story from the Community: Living the New Blueprint

Another client, Janelle, had been through childhood trauma and addiction recovery. When she completed the SEB Process, her vision wasn't about wealth or fame—it was about peace.

She shared that she used to wake up every morning with dread, her nervous system on high alert before the day even began. But after identifying and releasing the negative internal narratives, and reprogramming her mind to embrace the life she desired, she created a morning ritual of soft, sacred rhythm: prayer, breathwork, lighting a candle, and walking in nature barefoot when she could.

After several months of coaching together, one day she looked at me with tears in her eyes and said, "I love my life. I didn't know peace could be a habit."

That is the essence of recreation.

In this phase, you stop chasing the life you want—and start living it now. Not as a fantasy, but as a felt reality. One breath, one boundary, one conscious choice at a time.

The Science of Embodied Change

Dr. Candace Pert's research in psychoneuroimmunology suggests that every thought and emotion triggers a chemical cascade in the body. When you consistently think and feel from a new emotional state—such as gratitude, empowerment, or peace—you begin to recondition your body to a new baseline.

This is supported by Dr. Joe Dispenza's studies showing that sustained emotional coherence and elevated energy states not only change brain patterns but improve immune function and resilience.

In other words, the nervous system, endocrine system, and energy body will all begin to align with the vision you've claimed—as long as you live from it consistently.

The Slinky Spiral of Becoming

The recreation phase is not linear because healing is a spiral. You may revisit fear, doubt, or old triggers multiple times—but each time will be from a higher vantage point.

Like a slinky circling downward and upward simultaneously, you'll return to familiar terrain with new insight. You'll grieve again—but with more grace. You'll doubt again—but with deeper faith.

This is not regression. It's refinement.

Dr. Brené Brown, author of *The Gifts of Imperfection*, calls this the "rumble with vulnerability"—the continued practice of showing up as your full self, even when it's uncomfortable. In her work on wholeheartedness, she affirms that courage isn't just a one-time decision. It's a daily practice.

Recreation, then, is the practice of remembering who you are and choosing to live from that place—again and again.

Conclusion: Embodying the New Blueprint

Recreation is the exhale of the healing process. It's where theory becomes life, and life becomes truth. You're no longer just visualizing or reprogramming. Now, you're living as the embodied architect of your future—and that changes everything.

Because embodiment is not the end of your journey; it's the beginning of conscious creation. In the next chapter, we'll explore how to sustain and expand your transformation—so the life you've created doesn't just evolve, but thrives.

The proof of transformation isn't in what you've learned—it's in how you now live.

Deep Dive Practice: Living the Life You've Built

1. What would change if you made decisions from your future self's mindset every day?
2. Where are you still waiting for permission to live freely and fully?
3. What daily rituals or boundaries would honor the woman you're becoming?
4. How do you respond when your new identity feels untested or vulnerable—and what would courage look like instead?
5. What relationships, environments, or behaviors still reflect an outdated version of you—and how can you lovingly release or redefine them?
6. How will you celebrate your transformation in ways that honor both your becoming and your being?

"You are not just empowered. You are encoded with possibility. Live like the universe remembers you... Because it does."

~Dr. Sue Carter Collins

The Shift From Insight to Installation

The second phase of the Self-Empowerment Breakthrough Process™ guided you beyond awareness into the sacred work of internal rewiring. If Part I illuminated the patterns, Part II initiated the deep transformational shift. You began dismantling the architecture of the false self and building a foundation aligned with your divine identity.

You learned:

- **Reflecting** is the beginning of self-honesty. It is the sacred pause that allows you to witness your programming without shame, observe your patterns without judgment, and reclaim your power through conscious awareness. This phase asked you to see clearly—because what you refuse to face, you cannot change.
- **Reimagining** isn't about escape—it's about re-anchoring to truth. Vision is not fantasy; it is a memory of what your soul already knows is possible. You were invited to re-script your inner narrative and choose a future rooted in divine possibility, not conditioned fear.

- **Releasing** is not weakness—it's sacred surrender. You confronted the emotional weight, neural wiring, and energetic residue of old stories that no longer serve you. You honored the parts of you that survived and chose to let go of the identities that were never meant to stay.
- **Reprogramming** taught you how to shift from desire to design. Through neuroscience, repetition, and spiritual alignment, you began the daily process of wiring new beliefs into your subconscious. You became both the architect and the embodiment of your inner transformation.
- **Recreating** invited you to live the life your soul designed. This is where healing becomes habit—the daily devotion to walking in your vision, not as a goal but as a practiced identity. You began learning how to sustain your power without performing for it.

Part II reminded you that insight without integration leaves you circling the same mountain. Real transformation lives in repetition, embodiment, and practice—and none of it is linear.

Like the sacred slinky spiral, you will revisit lessons at deeper levels as you evolve. You will be called again and again to reflect, release, reimagine, reprogram, and recreate your life. This is not regression; it is divine refinement.

As we prepare to enter *Part III*, remember: mastery is not perfection. It is presence, alignment, and conscious choice—again and again. Here, you'll learn to translate mastery into motion: how to sustain your transformation, embody emotional intelligence, and live with grounded spiritual power in every dimension of your life.

You are not just breaking through.
You are becoming the woman you choose to be.

147

---

*"Integration is not an event—it is a becoming.
You don't just learn the truth. You practice it until
it lives in your bones."*
~Dr. Sue Carter Collins

PART III

Mind Mastery in Action

This final part is where inner transformation meets outer expression. Having learned to release, rewire, and realign, you now begin the art of living as your reimagined self.

Mind mastery in action is not about control—it's about coherence. It's the daily practice of listening deeply, choosing consciously, and walking in alignment with your divine intelligence.

Here, mastery becomes motion. You no longer strive to become her—you live as her. And through that embodiment, your life becomes the proof of what's possible.

Chapter 13

Intuition – Living in Divine Alignment

*"Intuition is the voice of divine alignment—
quiet, unshakable, and always faithful to your
highest truth."*

~ Dr. Sue Carter Collins

Trusting Your Inner Compass

You've done the deep work. You've reflected, reimagined, released, reprogrammed, and begun to recreate your life. Now, as you step into your reimagined self, one vital component must become central to your journey: intuition.

Intuition is the compass that guides you in alignment with your highest path. It is the bridge between your human logic and divine wisdom.

To live your reimagined life, you must be able to discern between the voice of fear and the voice of truth. You must recognize when you are being led by habit or history—versus when you are being called by Spirit.

This chapter is about learning to make a divine appointment with Source.
To sit in the silence.
To "stay in the ask."
To listen, hear, and trust your inner knowing.

What Is Intuition, Really?

Intuition is the voice of divine intelligence filtered through your soul. It doesn't arise from rational deduction or linear thinking—it rises from within you, often without explanation, yet with unmistakable clarity.

From a scientific perspective, intuition is a natural form of pattern recognition that occurs beneath conscious awareness. Your brain is constantly scanning and processing information—linking emotional memory, sensory patterns, and prior experiences—long before your conscious mind can make sense of them. These subtle signals are synthesized in the areas of the brain that integrate emotion and logic, guiding you toward rapid, experience-based decisions.

In other words, your *gut feeling* is not guesswork—it's intelligence. Your nervous system is an exquisite instrument of awareness, finely tuned to detect subtle cues about what feels safe, true, or aligned.

This is also why intuition is often felt in the body before it's understood by the mind. Those physical sensations—the quickening in your heart, the flutter in your stomach, the calm that washes over you—

are more than emotions. They are messages from your internal guidance system, what some scientists call "somatic markers," formed through emotional memory and lived experience.

Yet intuition is more than biology. It is also energetic and spiritual. Across metaphysical traditions, intuition is understood as the language of the soul—the way your Higher Self or Spirit communicates with you. It may arrive as a whisper, a nudge, a vivid image, or a quiet certainty that defies logic. Often, it bypasses words altogether and speaks through resonance, through what simply *feels right*.

Throughout the ages, spiritual teachers and philosophers have offered their own descriptions of this sacred intelligence.
Florence Scovel Shinn called it "the spiritual faculty that doesn't explain; it simply points the way."
Ernest Holmes described it as "Spirit in us revealing Itself to us."
Charles Fillmore taught that intuition is the wisdom of the heart—a sacred, innate intelligence beyond logic.
Dr. Wayne Dyer said, "If prayer is you talking to God, then intuition is God talking to you."
Michael Bernard Beckwith described it as "the receiver of the divine broadcast."
Even Carl Jung, the Swiss psychiatrist, believed intuition to be one of the four primary ways humans perceive reality, calling it "perception via the unconscious."

So intuition is not false, and it's not fantasy.
It is a form of higher intelligence that bridges science and spirit—a sacred partnership between divine wisdom and human design that scientists are only just beginning to understand.

Pause & Reflect: When have you recently felt a "knowing" that defied logic yet proved true? How did your body signal that inner truth before your mind caught up?

Signs You're Tuning In

Every person connects with their intuition differently, and no two inner languages sound exactly the same. Still, there are universal indicators that you're beginning to trust your inner compass rather than overriding it with logic or fear.

You sense truth without needing proof.
You may not be able to explain *how* you know something, yet the knowing feels solid and unmistakable. It's not wishful thinking; it's a quiet certainty that settles in your body like peace.

You feel "off" when something doesn't align—even if it looks good on paper.
Your intuition will often register discord before your mind can articulate why. You might feel tension in your chest, a knot in your stomach, or a sudden heaviness that says, *this isn't for me.*

You make decisions more easily, with less overthinking.
As you strengthen intuitive trust, the endless pros-and-cons lists start to fade. Choices feel cleaner, simpler, and guided by an inner clarity that needs no external validation.

You experience synchronicities or "divine winks" that confirm your path.

Unexpected alignments—meeting the right person at the right time, hearing a phrase you'd just prayed about, or seeing repeated numbers or symbols—become signposts reminding you that Spirit is partnering with you.

You feel guided—not driven.
Instead of hustling or forcing outcomes, you sense a natural rhythm to your actions. There's less striving and more flow, as though life itself is participating in your unfolding.

This connection is not magic—it is resonance.
As your energy becomes more coherent and your nervous system learns to rest in trust, your perception sharpens. You begin to distinguish the subtle difference between fear and truth, impulse and inspiration, urgency and divine timing. The more attuned you become, the more easily you recognize what expands your spirit— and what constricts it.

Pause & Reflect: Listening Between the Lines

Take a moment to recall a time when you sensed something before you *knew* it logically.

- How did that intuitive nudge show up—in your body, emotions, or environment?
- What happened when you followed it?
- What happened when you didn't?

Notice the patterns. Your intuition has always been speaking; you're simply learning its language.

Why Intuition Is Essential for Mind Mastery

Without intuition, you default to overthinking. Overthinking is the mind trying to lead without spiritual wisdom. Intuition is wisdom applied. It helps you make aligned decisions without overanalyzing every detail. It is the conduit between what your soul knows and what your mind can trust.

Cognitive science confirms that rational thinking is limited by working-memory capacity and shaped by prior biases—a finding popularized by psychologist Daniel Kahneman in his research on decision-making and intuitive judgment. In contrast, intuitive processing can bypass these constraints by synthesizing vast amounts of data quickly and holistically.

Intuition is clearest when your emotional body is regulated. Emotional reactivity can distort intuitive clarity, making fear feel like warning or urgency feel like truth. The more calm and centered you are, the more easily you can distinguish divine knowing from emotional noise.

But the deeper reason intuition matters is this: it is how your soul steers your mind.
True mind mastery is not about rigid logic—it's about inner congruence. When your intuition, body, and conscious mind are aligned, your choices become more resonant, expansive, and in harmony with your divine assignment.

Intuition is also a function of reprogramming. The more you clear limiting beliefs and trauma-based patterns, the more clearly your intuitive voice emerges. Your signal gets stronger. Your channel becomes clearer.

A Personal Story: Learning to Trust the Whisper

There was a time when I doubted every decision I made. I would analyze every angle, poll everyone I knew, and second-guess myself into paralysis. I wanted to be absolutely sure that I was making the right decision. I trusted everyone but myself. When the quiet voice of intuition came, I doubted it. I told myself I was just making things up. But here's what I had to learn:

Intuition doesn't shout. It whispers.

So I began to listen.

It was in the quiet moments—after meditation, during walks, while in prayer—that I began to hear that whisper. It wasn't loud, but it was unmistakably wise. And the answer—regardless of how I framed the question—was always the same. You see, this is the difference between divine intuition and the egoic mind. An ego-driven response may change from moment to moment, but divine intuition never wavers.

One time, I was offered a lucrative coaching opportunity with a prominent entrepreneur. On paper, it looked like a dream. I could make $5000 for a weekend of work. All I had to do was listen and talk. Who wouldn't jump at that offer? But every time I thought about it, my chest tightened and my energy contracted. I prayed, journaled, and consulted my inner knowing—and still, the answer was *no.*

So what did I do? I'd like to say that I declined, but the truth is that I went against my inner knowing and accepted the offer. The first day of the coaching session was great. The second day was a disaster. Although I had done my due diligence in asking if she was under medical supervision—she said no—it didn't take long to realize that she had been untruthful. As we proceeded with the coaching session, I became aware that she was exhibiting multiple personalities. This is the danger my Higher Self was trying to alert me to. I am an experienced life coach—I am not a mental-health therapist. I am not trained to deal with mental-health issues.

I learned a lot from that experience. I learned not to be taken in by the lure of money. I learned that not all clients are my clients and not all money is good money. Mostly, I learned to listen and follow my intuition.

That experience changed me at my spiritual core. I began to trust the knowing inside me, even when it defied reason. Even when it disappointed others. Even when I couldn't explain it.
And that trust continues to shape my life today in powerful ways.

Pause & Reflect: When has your intuition spoken clearly to you—and how did you respond? What did that experience teach you about trusting yourself?

Client Story: Tamika's Intuitive Rebirth

Tamika was a data analyst—rational, brilliant, and methodical. She came to coaching because she felt "stuck" despite achieving everything she thought she wanted.

As we worked together, she revealed that she'd always dreamed of opening her own business—but dismissed it as "unrealistic." Her intuition had whispered for years, but she'd silenced it in favor of logic.

One day, during a visioning meditation, she had a powerful emotional release. Tears streamed down her face as she said aloud, "I want to build something that heals."

Within six months, Tamika resigned from her job, enrolled in holistic-health training, and began hosting pop-up wellness events. Her energy shifted and her joy returned. She wasn't chasing success anymore. She was following her soul.

How to Strengthen Your Intuition

There are many ways to strengthen your intuition. These are some that are effective:

1. **Create Sacred Stillness**
   Intuition speaks in silence. Begin a daily practice of meditation, nature walks, or silent mornings. Stillness is not passive—it is where your inner voice becomes audible.

2. **Ask Empowering Questions**
   Stay in the ask. Start your day with: "What do I need to know today?" or "What would my higher self do?" Then listen. The answer may come as a thought, a feeling, or a sign.

3. **Journal Your Inner Nudges**
   Keep an intuition journal. Track the hunches, dreams, gut feelings, and synchronicities you experience. Pattern recognition is the path to trust.

4. **Feel Before You Think**

   Before making a decision, drop into your body. Does your energy expand or contract? Does your chest open or tighten? Your body is a truth-teller—don't ignore it.

5. **Act on the Nudge**

   Intuition becomes stronger with action. Each time you follow it, even in small ways, you strengthen the connection between your inner wisdom and outer reality.

Why This Matters for Your Reimagined Life

To live as your reimagined self, you must move in partnership with the divine. You are no longer just strategizing—you are surrendering. You are no longer just doing—you are discerning. You are no longer just planning—you are listening.

Intuition is the muscle of alignment.
It helps you navigate uncertainty with grace.
It anchors your decisions in soul wisdom.
It keeps you in tune with your highest vibration.

When you trust your intuition, you no longer have to push or prove. You flow. You align. You become magnetic—not because you hustle, but because you harmonize.
You stop chasing answers.
You start living from the truth already inside you.

Conclusion: From Listening To Living

You are already wired to receive divine guidance.

You don't have to chase it, prove yourself worthy of it, or fear that it will leave you. The signal has always been there—you're simply learning to tune to its frequency.

The more you trust your inner knowing, the more life confirms that you are on the right path. Each act of trust strengthens your alignment. Each moment of surrender amplifies your connection to Source.

You are not walking this journey alone. Your soul is always speaking. Your job is to listen—and follow the whisper that leads you home to yourself.

As you move forward, you'll see how this inner alignment becomes the foundation for everything you create next. Because when intuition leads, life unfolds with precision and purpose.

Next, we'll explore how to turn this divine alignment into daily action—how to embody intuitive flow as you navigate the outer world of creation, leadership, and manifestation.

You are not just guided—you are divinely aligned.

Deep Dive Practice: Listening for the Whisper

1. When have I allowed fear or logic to drown out the whisper of divine guidance—and what did that experience teach me about trust?
2. What decision in my life right now is asking for deeper intuitive listening?
3. What would shift in my life if I chose to seek divine guidance and act on intuitive nudges more consistently?
4. What does an intuitive "yes" feel like in my body—and how do I recognize a "no"?
5. What old belief or habit do I need to release in order to fully trust my inner wisdom?

"You are not lost. You are being led. Trust the whisper.
It knows the way."

~ Dr. Sue Carter Collins

Chapter 14

Emotional Mastery – Living With Awareness, Not Reaction

"Emotional mastery is not about becoming invulnerable—it's about becoming so present, so rooted in truth, that nothing can pull you out of alignment with your power."

~ Dr. Sue Carter Collins

Becoming the Witness of Your Truth

You've learned to listen, to trust, and to live from divine alignment. Yet even alignment must be sustained. To remain rooted in your power, another inner gate must be crossed—the gate of emotional mastery.

This chapter is not about suppressing your emotions or bypassing discomfort; it is about learning how to be with your emotions—without being ruled by them. It is about becoming the witness, the container, and the transformer of your inner world so that external circumstances no longer dictate your internal reality.

This is where mind mastery moves from concept to realization.

What Is Emotional Mastery?

Emotional mastery is the ability to respond to your emotions rather than react from them. It means feeling your feelings fully without letting them drive your decisions, shape your identity, or derail your peace.

It is not about denying pain, numbing sadness, or forcing yourself into positivity. It's about developing the awareness, regulation, and resilience to move through emotion consciously, instead of being swept away by it unconsciously.

While much attention in personal development is given to rewiring thought patterns, your emotions are often the true architects of your experience. They shape what you notice, how you react, what you remember, and what you come to believe is possible. If thoughts are the blueprint, emotions are the builders—and your nervous system is the construction site.

Psychologist Daniel Goleman's research on emotional intelligence identifies four key capacities shared by emotionally intelligent individuals: self-awareness, self-regulation, social awareness, and relationship management. His findings show that people with high EQ are more successful in leadership, relationships, and overall well-being—not because they avoid emotions, but because they understand and manage them skillfully.

From a neuroscience perspective, emotional mastery involves integration between the prefrontal cortex (the thinking brain) and the limbic system (the emotional brain)—particularly the amygdala, which is responsible for processing threat and emotion. When the amygdala hijacks the nervous system, you experience reactivity, fight-or-flight responses, or emotional overwhelm. However, when the prefrontal cortex is engaged, you gain access to choice, reflection, and regulation.

Metaphysically Speaking

Emotional mastery is about becoming the observer rather than the reactor. In many mystical traditions—from Buddhism to Hermeticism to New Thought—emotions are seen as energy in motion (*e-motion*), rising and falling like waves. You are not the wave—you are the ocean.

Spiritual teachers such as Abraham-Hicks describe unprocessed emotional energy as vibrational clutter—distortions that block your energetic flow and delay manifestations. Florence Scovel Shinn captured this truth when she wrote, *"Fear is only inverted faith. It is faith in evil instead of good."*

When you suppress emotions, you suppress energy. When you avoid feeling, you obstruct healing. To master your emotions is to reclaim your energetic sovereignty; to clean your vibrational field and make your nervous system a safe place for your soul to live.

Pause & Reflect: When uncomfortable emotions arise, do you allow them to move through you—or do you try to manage, fix, or avoid them? What might shift if you simply witnessed the feeling without resistance?

When Emotion Becomes Identity

Many of us were taught to be strong, to hold it together, or to get over it. As a result, we never learned to feel safely. We stuffed our sadness, masked our anger, and pretended away our fear. Because we didn't learn to feel emotions cleanly, we began to internalize them.

Here are some examples:

- "I feel rejected" became "I am unlovable."
- "I feel overwhelmed" became "I'm not capable."
- "I feel afraid" became "I'm weak."

These identity statements become ingrained beliefs—ones that operate beneath awareness and shape your self-concept, behaviors, and decisions.

Healing begins when you recognize:
Emotions are merely messengers; they are not definitions.
You are not your fear. You are not your sadness. You are not your anger.
You are the one experiencing it—and that means you have the power to move through it.

Sandi's Story: The Woman She Almost Forgot

During one coaching session, Sandi, a professional woman in her mid-30s, broke down in tears.
"I don't know who I am anymore," she said. "I used to be confident. I used to light up every room. Now, I just… hold everything in."

As we explored her feelings, it became clear that Sandi had internalized decades of emotional messages. She had been told as a child to stop crying, to be "the strong one," to never let people see her fall apart… and she didn't.

But in hiding her emotions, she had also hidden herself.

When we began doing somatic work, she realized that her body had become a container for everything she'd never said: the grief from a miscarriage, the rage from a betrayal, the fear of never being enough.

Bit by bit, she began to reclaim her voice—not by pushing through emotion, but by honoring it. She learned to breathe through the discomfort, to name what she was feeling, and to express herself with integrity.

"I'm not afraid of my feelings anymore," she said one day. "They're not in control of me—I'm in conversation with them."

That is emotional mastery.

Pause & Reflect: When have you silenced an emotion to keep the peace or protect an image? How might your healing deepen if you gave that feeling a safe voice today?

How the Body Holds Emotion

Emotions are not just mental phenomena—they are somatic. The body stores unprocessed emotions in the nervous system, fascia, and cellular memory. Trauma researcher Bessel van der Kolk explains that trauma and unhealed emotion are physically imprinted in the body, often leading to chronic tension, pain, fatigue, and disease.

This is why healing cannot happen only through cognitive insight. It must include nervous-system regulation and emotional release.

When you master your emotions, you become fluent in the language of your body. You notice the subtle signals—tight shoulders, shallow breath, clenching jaws—and respond before the emotion becomes dysregulation or disease.

Tools for Emotional Mastery

There are numerous tools that can be used effectively to facilitate emotional mastery. Here are a few evidence-based and spiritually grounded practices:

- **Mindful Awareness** – Learn to observe your emotions without judgment. Practice saying: "I'm noticing that I feel anxious," instead of "I am anxious." This subtle shift creates space between you and the emotion.
- **Somatic Grounding** – When emotions rise, place your hands on your body—over your heart, belly, or thighs. Feel the ground beneath you. Engage the senses: What do you

see, smell, feel, or hear? This brings the nervous system back to the present moment.

- **Breath Regulation** – Slow, deep breathing—especially through the nose and with long exhales—activates the parasympathetic nervous system (your body's rest-and-restore mode). Even three slow breaths can reset your emotional state.

- **Emotional Labeling (Name It to Tame It)** – Research shows that naming your emotion reduces amygdala activity. Say out loud: "This is sadness." "This is frustration." "This is fear." When you name it, you tame it.

- **The Power of the Pause** – A conscious pause can interrupt automatic patterns. Breathwork—such as box breathing (inhale 4, hold 4, exhale 4, hold 4)—can calm the vagus nerve and help restore internal balance.

- **Conscious Expression** – Give your emotions safe expression. Journal, move your body, cry, scream into a pillow, speak your truth. Let the energy move through you rather than calcify inside you.

- **Emotional Alchemy** – From a metaphysical perspective, emotions can be transmuted through practices like intention setting, prayer, sacred movement, and embodiment. You can turn grief into gratitude, anger into clarity, and fear into faith.

- **Metacognition** – This is the practice of thinking about your thinking. When you can step outside your own thoughts and observe your emotional patterns, you gain perspective—and with perspective comes choice.

Pause & Reflect: Practicing Emotional Mastery

Take a moment to pause before moving forward.
Close your eyes. Inhale slowly through your nose, exhale through your mouth, and allow your body to settle. Notice what emotions are present right now—no judgment, just awareness.

Now consider:

1. Which of the emotional mastery tools you've learned so far have you actually tried in real life? What was your experience with them?
2. When you notice emotional triggers arise, which practice helps you return to center most effectively?
3. Choose one new tool or technique from this chapter that you are willing to try today. How will you remind yourself to use it when the next challenge appears?

Emotional mastery grows through practice. Each conscious breath, each intentional pause, each moment of self-awareness is a step toward calm becoming your new normal.

Why This Matters for Mind Mastery

Mind mastery is knowing when to pause, when to speak, when to feel, and when to let go.

You can't create a new life with an unregulated nervous system. You can't access divine wisdom while trapped in emotional reactivity. And you can't follow your intuition while suppressing the truth of how you feel.

The more you master your emotions, the more you reclaim your energy. In doing so, you stop leaking power in conflict, fear, or overreaction. You start responding from truth, not trauma. You become the calm in the storm—not because you avoid emotion, but because you've mastered the art of riding the waves.

Conclusion: From Reaction to Reverence

Emotional mastery doesn't mean you never get upset. It means you know how to return to yourself—again and again.

You become less reactive, more responsive. Less triggered, more centered. Less afraid of your own depth—and more in tune with the wisdom it holds.

When you master your emotions, you no longer live at their mercy.
You live from your power.
You live from your truth.
You live from awareness—not reaction.

As you continue your journey, you'll discover that emotional steadiness is not about control—it's about reverence. Reverence for your humanity, for your process, and for the divine intelligence that animates every feeling.

Next, we'll explore how this reverence transforms relationships, leadership, and service—where emotional wisdom becomes a vessel for authentic connection and compassionate influence.

You are not ruled by emotion; you are refined by it.

Deep Dive Practice: Living With Emotional Wisdom

1. What was my earliest memory of being told to suppress or hide emotion?
2. How do I tend to react when I feel overwhelmed, rejected, or unseen?
3. How do I distinguish between reacting from pain and responding from truth?
4. What emotions do I most often resist—and why?
5. What tools or practices help me feel safe expressing my emotions?

"Emotional mastery is not about becoming invulnerable—it's about becoming so present, so rooted in truth, that nothing can pull you out of alignment with your power."

~ Dr. Sue Carter Collins

Chapter 15

The Liberated Self – Embodying the Truth of Who You Are

"The Liberated Self is not who you become—it is who you remember. It rises when you finally stop trying to be who the world told you to be."

~ Dr. Sue Carter Collins

When the False Self Dissolves

You've learned to master your emotions and anchor in inner peace. Now it's time to live from that peace—to let your wholeness lead. You've done the work—not just the outer work of shifting behaviors, but the deep internal excavation—the remembering, reprogramming, and reclamation of who you truly are.

You've learned to listen to your intuition. You've mastered the ability to become the calm within. Now comes the embodiment.

This chapter is not about doing more. It is about becoming more of who you already are.

Liberation is not something you seek.
It is something you allow.

The Liberated Self is not a persona you create—it is the divine self you uncover when the false self is dissolved. It's what rises when shame, fear, guilt, and approval-seeking fall away. It is what breathes through you when your soul is no longer silenced by survival strategies.

You do not earn your liberation.
You embody it.

For liberation is a process, not a destination.
It requires commitment and devotion.
The work is hard.
And the results are worth it.

But What Is Liberation, Really?

In psychological terms, liberation refers to release from limiting beliefs, roles, and conditioning that keep us bound to disempowering patterns. It often parallels what psychologist Abraham Maslow described as *self-actualization*—living in alignment with one's inner truth, creativity, autonomy, and purpose. But true freedom goes even deeper.

In spiritual traditions, liberation is called *moksha* in Hinduism, *nirvana* in Buddhism, and *salvation* in Christian mysticism—a state of union with the Divine, freedom from illusion, and embodiment of truth.

From a metaphysical perspective, liberation is the return to wholeness. It is remembering that you are not your story. You are not your trauma. You are not even your identity as you've known it. You are a spiritual being encoded with divine intelligence, worthy of love, joy, and sovereignty by design—not by achievement.

Liberation is not perfection.
It is permission.
It is transformation.

The False Self vs. the Liberated Self

The **False Self** is formed in reaction to pain. It is the mask you wear to protect the parts of you that were never fully seen, accepted, or celebrated.

- It performs.
- It conforms.
- It over-functions.
- It shrinks.
- It strives to earn what you were born worthy of.

The **Liberated Self** is the soul in its natural state—whole, wise, intuitive, powerful, and free.

- It leads with truth, not fear.
- It honors boundaries without guilt.
- It creates from overflow, not lack.
- It speaks with clarity and love.
- It knows that being is enough.

Your false self may have helped you survive.
But your Liberated Self will help you thrive.

Pause & Reflect: Which aspects of your life are still being shaped by the false self's need for approval or safety? What would shift if you led with the wholeness of your Liberated Self instead?

The Neuroscience of Liberation

Transformation requires neuroplasticity—the brain's ability to rewire itself through new thoughts, behaviors, and emotional responses. The more you practice new ways of being, the more the old identity dissolves.

When you act from your Liberated Self—setting boundaries, speaking truth, choosing joy—you create new neural pathways that anchor this identity into your nervous system. Over time, your brain stops defaulting to survival patterns and begins supporting your freedom.

This is how identity becomes embodiment: through consistent alignment between thought, emotion, and action.

Staying Rewired – Becoming Your New Default

You didn't arrive at liberation by accident. It was a choice—repeated, intentional, sacred. If you want to stay rewired, that choice must become ingrained.

Neuroscience shows that the brain prunes unused neural pathways while strengthening those used repeatedly. So, while your Liberated Self may feel natural now, it still requires reinforcement to become your default identity.

This is not about striving; it is about consistency.

To stay rewired, you must:

- Keep showing up as her, even when old patterns try to re-emerge.
- Pause and breathe before reacting—especially when triggered.
- Anchor your mornings in soul-alignment before the world demands your attention.
- Speak your truth even when your voice trembles.
- Choose alignment over autopilot, again and again.

Liberation is not one grand moment of freedom. It is a daily devotion to embodying the truth you've reclaimed.

Over time, you'll notice: the old self doesn't vanish with force—it simply fades from lack of attention. The more you invest in your inner freedom, the more magnetic, grounded, and alive you become.

Pause & Reflect: What daily rituals or practices help you stay anchored in your Liberated Self, especially when old patterns whisper for attention?

Energetic Alignment and Frequency Liberation

Heart-brain coherence research from Gregg Braden and the HeartMath Institute demonstrates that harmony between the heart and mind produces energetic alignment—a physiological state where the body's electromagnetic field becomes more coherent and ordered.

The Liberated Self is a frequency; when you live in that frequency, your outer world must rearrange to match it.

In other words, you don't wait to be free. You live free—and watch everything else align.

Living as the Liberated Self

Arriving at this stage does not mean you will never feel fear, doubt, or grief. It means you no longer let them take the wheel.

You start making choices from alignment, not anxiety.
You build relationships based on resonance, not rescue.
You show up in the world with integrity, not performance.

- You speak your truth without apology or aggression.
- You say *no* without guilt—and *yes* without self-abandonment.
- You stop waiting for permission and start embodying possibility.
- You choose ease without shame and power without control.
- You create, connect, and contribute from a place of inner fullness.
- You allow joy, rest, and radiance to be part of your rhythm—not just your productivity.

You don't become a different person.

You become you—unfiltered, unhidden, and unleashed.

Always ready to embrace life with gratitude—the highest frequency possible.

Pause & Reflect: Where in my life am I still operating from the false self—performing, pleasing, or striving for approval?

Why This Matters for Mind Mastery

Mind mastery isn't just about managing thoughts. It's about reclaiming identity.

If you change habits but remain bound to an outdated self-image, you'll sabotage your progress.

If you learn the tools but still feel unworthy of freedom, you'll recreate the very cycles you worked so hard to escape.

When you live as the Liberated Self, your thoughts, emotions, and behaviors flow from truth.

You're not pushing against yourself—you're partnering with your soul.

You're not seeking worthiness—you're expressing it.

Your expression doesn't remove you from responsibility; it grounds you in it—with more clarity, compassion, and capacity to serve without self-erasure.

This is what it means to embrace your authentic self—to live from the inside out.

From Healing to Wholeness

The Liberated Self is your truest self—beneath the masks, beyond the trauma, and before the world asked you to shrink.

So remember this:
You don't have to earn your freedom. You simply have to stop abandoning it.
You don't have to become someone else to be powerful. You simply have to reconnect with who you were before the world told you who to be.
You don't have to heal every wound to be whole. You simply have to stop confusing your scars with your identity.

You are ready. Ready to live.
Not because everything is perfect,
but because your truth can no longer wait.

It's your time to stand in your power.
It's your time to embrace your purpose.
It's your time to live free—as your Liberated Self.

Next, we'll explore how living as your Liberated Self naturally expands into leadership, service, and legacy—where your personal freedom becomes a source of empowerment for others.

You are not becoming free; you are remembering that you already are.

Deep Dive Practice: Living as the Liberated Self

1. What does my Liberated Self know to be true about me that I often forget?
2. How does my body feel when I am in alignment with truth versus when I am in survival mode?
3. Which daily practices help strengthen the new neural pathways of freedom and authenticity?
4. What situations tend to pull me back into old patterns—and how can I pause and re-center in those moments?

"Liberation isn't loud. It's steady. It's the quiet, embodied knowing. I am enough. I am free. I am whole."
~ Dr. Sue Carter Collins

Chapter 16

Living on Purpose – Leading With Soul

*"Purpose is not a performance.
It is a soul agreement — a sacred yes to
becoming who you truly are."*

~ Dr. Sue Carter Collins

Embodiment Is the Goal

You've learned to live as your Liberated Self — anchored in inner peace and truth. Now comes the sacred question: **How will you live it?**

This chapter is not about productivity; it is about embodiment. Not performance, striving, or proving — but living with purpose in a way that is resonant, rooted, and real.

To live on purpose is to anchor your inner transformation into outer expression. It means your values are no longer theoretical; they shape your choices. Your energy is no longer scattered by urgency — it is devoted to what expands your soul. And most of all, you are no longer chasing meaning.
You are becoming it.

What Does It Mean to Live on Purpose?

Purpose is not a destination, a five-year plan, or a title. It is a state of alignment — a way of being in which your inner truth and outer life are congruent. It often emerges not from ease, but from disruption — through breakdowns, quiet nudges, and divine detours that won't let you rest in mediocrity.

Living on purpose means:

- Your being and doing are in harmony.
- Your choices reflect your truth.
- Your work carries meaning beyond the paycheck.
- Your relationships elevate, not exhaust, your energy.
- Your existence becomes a blessing, not a performance.

Psychologist Abraham Maslow described the pinnacle of human potential as self-actualization — the realization of one's gifts and fulfillment. Later he added a sixth stage: *self-transcendence.* That is where purpose truly lives — not in personal success alone, but in contributing that success toward something greater.

Self-transcendence is not martyrdom. It is the movement from ego identity to soul identity. You stop asking, "What can I get from the world?" and start asking, "What can I give to the world from the fullness of who I am?"

The Energetics of Purpose

From a metaphysical lens, purpose is not a role you play — it is a frequency you emit. It is the vibration of your being when you are living in truth.

Spiritual teacher Michael Beckwith reminds us that purpose is encoded in the soul; it is not figured out through logic but revealed through spiritual visioning. Research by Gregg Braden and the HeartMath Institute shows that heart-brain coherence — the alignment of our cognitive, emotional, and intuitive systems — creates resonance that allows higher insight and creativity to emerge.

Neville Goddard taught that we must "assume the feeling of the wish fulfilled." Purpose isn't something that will arrive once life is perfect; it unfolds now, as you embody the woman you were created to be.

When you live on purpose, you become a vibrational match for what is already yours. You stop forcing alignment and start living in agreement with your divine assignment.

Pause & Reflect: What does alignment feel like in your body when you are living your truth? Where in your life do you sense the need for realignment?

You Are Not Behind

One of the biggest lies propounded is that you are "too late." That you missed the moment. That someone else already did what you were meant to do.

But the truth is this: You are not late.
You are becoming — and your becoming is right on time.

Divine timing does not follow the world's clock. It includes every lesson, detour, heartbreak, and healing that shaped your character. It includes the nights you cried out for direction and the mornings you still chose to rise.

Sometimes purpose hides in quiet roles, unseen choices, and resilience no one applauds.
Purpose is not an exit strategy. It is a sacred remembering.
And you are not late. You are right on schedule.

Purpose in Practice

Purpose doesn't always arrive with fanfare. Sometimes it reveals itself in quiet decisions no one sees. It's not always glamorous — but it's always true.

Living on purpose may require you to:

- Say no to opportunities that look good but feel off.
- Leave roles that no longer match your identity.
- Speak truth in rooms where you once stayed small.
- Choose alignment over applause.
- Serve in ways that stretch your comfort — but not your soul.

Theologian Frederick Buechner wrote, *"Vocation is the place where your deep gladness and the world's deep hunger meet."*
That is purpose — not performance, but soul service.

Pause & Reflect: What decisions or patterns are quietly asking to be realigned with your deeper truth? How might saying a sacred no create space for a truer yes?

Integration Is a Lifestyle

Living on purpose isn't a one-time breakthrough. It's a lived frequency.

The mind you've rewired — the identity you've reclaimed — needs daily nurturing to stay clear and connected. Otherwise, old paradigms can resurface under stress or uncertainty.

That's why integration is not an afterthought; it is the practice. Ask yourself daily:

- Is my inner truth leading this decision?
- Does this yes honor the woman I've become — or the one I used to be?
- Am I creating from overflow, or trying to prove I'm enough?
- Is my nervous system calm? Is my soul at peace?

These questions are not tests. They are tools of alignment. They help you recalibrate—not from pressure, but from presence. Integration is not perfection. It is remembrance.

Staying rewired means staying willing — to pause, to listen, to lead from soul instead of survival.

A Personal Story: I Thought I Had Missed It

There was a time when I thought I had waited too long. I had followed the script and obtained the degrees, accolades, and leadership roles — but the script didn't fit my soul.

I remember watching other women thrive in their gifts—speaking, writing, leading—and thinking, *That should have been me.*

But Spirit disrupted that narrative.
First with a whisper.
Then with a nudge.
Then with a directive: "Feed my sheep."

This time, the command was louder. And that moment changed everything.

I realized that my purpose had never left me; it had waited until I became the woman who could hold it with integrity — not ego; devotion — not striving.
It didn't come when I wanted or how I expected.
But when it came, it was right on time.

Client Story: Denisha's Shift from Success to Significance

Denisha was a successful high-achieving woman with accolades and power—but no peace. She came to coaching not for strategy, but for soul clarity. "I have everything I thought I wanted," she said, "but none of it feels like me anymore."

As we worked together, she remembered how alive she felt mentoring young women earlier in her career. She wept—it felt like coming home.

Months later, she left her corporate job and founded a nonprofit for teen girls in underserved communities. She now wakes up with energy she thought she'd lost forever.

Denisha didn't find her purpose.
She remembered it.

Leading, Loving, and Serving from Overflow

When you live on purpose, your leadership expands. You don't lead to be seen; you lead to illuminate.

Your love matures. You love from wholeness, not need. You stop performing, fixing, or proving—and start creating sacred reciprocity.

Your service deepens. Whether on a stage or at a kitchen table, your presence becomes a ministry of alignment.

This is what it means to lead from overflow. You are not drained by giving. You are fueled by embodiment.

Pause & Reflect: Where am I being invited to lead, love, or serve from overflow instead of obligation?

Why This Matters for Mind Mastery

Mind mastery is not the absence of thought—it is the presence of clarity.

It is the ability to discern what is real, what is required, and what is aligned. When your inner truth becomes your outer life, you stop performing versions of yourself and start living as yourself.

You stop battling the gap between who you are and who you pretend to be.
You live in congruence.
You lead with clarity.
You move with purpose.

In that alignment, you become a force — quiet or bold, soft or strong — through which the Divine can freely flow.

From Alignment to Illumination

Your purpose is not something to be proven. It is something to be honored.

The more you align with it, the more your life becomes a reflection of who you truly are.

Let the doing arise from the being.
Let your decisions reflect your devotion.
Let your presence become the purpose.

You were not created to simply succeed.
You were created to illuminate the world.

Next, we'll step beyond the framework — into your lived legacy. The journey of mind mastery culminates not in knowledge, but in embodiment: where your life itself becomes the message.

You were never behind.

You were being prepared to shine.

Deep Dive Practice: Purpose in Motion

1. How has my understanding of purpose evolved through this journey of mind mastery?
2. Which areas of my life now feel most aligned with my soul — and which still feel performative or forced?
3. What truth am I ready to live, even if it disrupts expectations or disappoints others?
4. What small, unseen choices can I make daily that reflect my sacred assignment?

"Your purpose isn't waiting to be found. It is waiting to be lived.
And every aligned choice is a holy act of becoming."
~ Dr. Sue Carter Collins

From Practice to Power – Sustaining the Transformation

Part III marked your transition from inner recalibration to external mastery. You stepped into the realm of application—where all the insight, healing, and rewiring began to take shape in daily life. This was the movement from *"I understand"* to *"I choose differently."*

You learned how to:

- **Make decisions from alignment rather than fear.** You practiced pausing, checking in, and choosing from your Higher Self instead of default patterns. You reclaimed your authority over your choices.
- **Cultivate emotional mastery** by witnessing your feelings without being ruled by them. You discovered how to honor your emotions as sacred messengers while choosing empowered responses.
- **Speak with power and precision.** You explored the impact of language on identity and learned to use words that affirm your worth, declare your vision, and elevate your frequency.
- **Integrate everything you've learned.** You examined what it means to stay rewired—to keep walking the path when

life throws a curveball—and to embody mastery as a living process, not a destination.

This final phase of the journey reminded you that true transformation isn't measured by how much you know; it's measured by how well you live.
Every breath, every boundary, every word, and every choice is an opportunity to practice what you now believe. Mastery is not about being perfect—it's about being present and choosing, again and again, to align your life with your truth.

You are no longer becoming.
You are now living it.
And that changes everything.

As we move into the Epilogue, take a moment to honor the purpose that has been awakening within you. You have not only mastered your mind—you have begun to master your life. You have learned to live with intention, to choose from awareness, and to lead from authenticity. This is what self-empowerment truly means: living on purpose, in purpose, and as purpose.

The pages ahead are not an ending but an emergence—an invitation to embody your power, express your divine potential, and walk boldly into the world as the woman you were always meant to be.

"Mastery isn't about control. It's about alignment.
When your thoughts, actions, and energy tell the same
story, you become unstoppable."
~ Dr. Sue Carter Collins

EPILOGUE

LIVING AS THE MASTER OF YOUR MIND AND THE ARCHITECT OF YOUR LIFE

You have learned to live on purpose, in purpose, and as purpose. This is the essence of self-empowerment—the quiet confidence that rises when your inner world and outer life finally align. You are no longer seeking power outside yourself. You are living from it, as it, and through it.

You've looked within, peeled back the layers, challenged old conditioning, and released what no longer served you.
You've rewritten the stories that once kept you bound.
You've remembered who you are—not the woman the world tried to mold, but the woman your soul always knew was there.

You are no longer reacting—you are responding with clarity.
You are no longer performing—you are showing up with authenticity.
You are no longer chasing—you are attracting by divine frequency.

This is the embodiment of mind mastery.
Not as control.
Not as striving.
But as conscious creation.

You began this journey searching for something—tools, answers, healing, maybe even hope.

But what you discovered was far greater:

You are not broken.

You are not behind.

You are not too much, too late, or too far gone.

You are the miracle you were waiting for—the savior you dreamed of.

You are the living proof that it is possible to rewrite your story, reclaim your power, and rise into a life you love.

So walk with reverence.

Walk with power.

Walk as the woman who remembers her worth, her voice, her vision—and never gives them away again.

Live your reimagined life—out loud.

Not tomorrow.

Not when it's perfect.

Right now.

There's One More Sacred Truth You Should Know

You were always Her.

You were never broken.

You were becoming.

The woman you've reclaimed—the one who leads with wisdom, trusts her knowing, speaks her truth, honors her peace, and lives her purpose—was always there.

She was buried beneath roles.
Silenced by stories.
Concealed by survival.
But she never left.

She waited—patiently, fiercely, lovingly—for you to remember.
This journey wasn't about fixing what was wrong.
It was about uncovering what was true.
You didn't become someone new.
You became who you were always meant to be.

Through the lens of science, soul, and sacred practice, you've learned to understand your mind, master your emotions, rewire your beliefs, and co-create a life in divine alignment.
You've journeyed through the terrain of the subconscious.
Interrupted cycles of struggle.
Reprogrammed patterns of pain.
Chosen clarity over confusion.
Truth over trauma.
Alignment over approval.

And now, you lead—not from ego, but from essence.
You love—not from need, but from overflow.
You serve—not from obligation, but from divine assignment.

This book was never about giving you something you lacked.
It was about revealing what was always within you:
Wholeness.
Wisdom.
Sovereignty.

You've dismantled the cage.
You've rewritten the script.
You've remembered the truth of who you are.

This is not the end of your journey.
It is the beginning of your legacy.

Because when one woman rises in her truth, she doesn't rise alone.
She lifts generations with her.
She awakens others by her example.
She becomes the portal through which collective healing flows.

You are not a chapter.
You are the whole book—a sacred text written in fire, faith, and freedom.

You are not just empowered.
You are divinely aligned.
And your becoming was never about finding your worth.
It was about remembering that you always were—
Her.

So exhale.
You've done the work.
Now live the life—
freely, intentionally, and with unwavering grace—
as the woman who has mastered her mind
and is now, at last, **mastering her life.**

Benediction

To master your mind is to remember your divinity.
May your life be the evidence of your awakening.
May every step you take affirm your purpose,
every word you speak echo your truth,
and every life you touch feel the power of your
becoming.
~ Dr. Sue Carter Collins~
The Mind Mastery Architect™

A Note of Appreciation

To you—
the reader who chose this book, opened these pages, and stayed
the course...

Thank you.
You could have chosen anything else.
But you chose yourself.
You showed up.
You leaned in.
You listened.
You reflected.

And whether your transformation came as a slow, quiet unfolding
or a fierce, undeniable awakening—
you allowed the journey to move through you.

That is no small feat.
Transformation is holy work.
It takes courage to face your thoughts.
It takes strength to rewrite your story.
And it takes sacred intention to reclaim your power
and rise into your truth.

So I honor you—
for your hunger,
for your heart,
for your healing.

This book is now a part of your story—
and you are forever a part of mine.

With deepest gratitude,
Dr. Sue Carter Collins
The Mind Mastery Architect™

Acknowledgments

To my **Divine Spiritual Council**—the unseen teachers, wise elders, and radiant energies who whisper truth into my spirit—I honor your presence and guidance. You have walked with me through valleys, illuminated the path when I could not see, and reminded me of who I am when the world tried to make me forget. Thank you for speaking to me in dreams, signs, synchronicities, and sacred stillness.

To my **ancestors**—those whose names I know and those whose names I do not—you are the blood in my veins, the strength in my spine, and the fire in my voice. Thank you for surviving what I will never have to. Thank you for guiding my steps with the quiet power of your memory and the sacred call of your mission.

This book is not mine alone.
It is the culmination of lifetimes of remembering.
It is the fruit of prayers whispered across generations.
It is the offering I now place upon your altar—
with reverence, gratitude, and love.

References Cited

Barrett, L. F. (2020). *Seven and a half lessons about the brain.* Mariner Books.

Barrett, L. F. (2021, February 3). That is not how your brain works. *Nautilus.* https://nautil.us/that-is-n0ot-how-your-brain-works-238138/

Bechara, A., Damasio, H., Tranel, D., & Damasio, A. R. (1997). Deciding advantageously before knowing the advantageous strategy. *Science, 275*(5304), 1293–1295. https://doi.org/10.1126/science.275.5304.1293

Beck, A. T. (2008). The evolution of the cognitive model of depression and its neurobiological correlates. *American Journal of Psychiatry, 165*(8), 969–977. https://doi.org/10.1176/appi.ajp.2008.08050721

Beckwith, M. B. (2011). *Life visioning: A transformative process for activating your unique gifts and highest potential.* Sounds True.

Bowers, M. E., & Yehuda, R. (2016). Intergenerational transmission of stress in humans. *Neuropsychopharmacology, 41*(1), 232–244.

Braden, G. (2021). *The wisdom codes: Ancient words to rewire our brains and heal our hearts.* Hay House.

Brown, B. (2020). *The gifts of imperfection.* Hazelden. (Original work published 2010)

Clark, A. (2013). Whatever next? Predictive brains, situated agents, and the future of cognitive science. *Behavioral and Brain Sciences, 36*(3), 181–204. https://doi.org/10.1017/S0140525X12000477

Clear, J. (2018). *Atomic habits.* Avery.

DeCasper, A. J., & Spence, M. J. (1986). Prenatal maternal speech influences newborns' perception of speech sounds. *Infant Behavior and Development, 9*(2), 133–150. https://doi.org/10.1016/0163-6383(86)90025-1

Damasio, A. R. (1996). The somatic marker hypothesis and the possible functions of the prefrontal cortex. *Philosophical Transactions of the Royal Society of London. Series B: Biological Sciences, 351*(1346), 1413–1420. https://doi.org/10.1098/rstb.1996.0125

Dispenza, J. (2012). *Breaking the habit of being yourself: How to lose your mind and create a new one.* Hay House.

Doidge, N. (2007). *The brain that changes itself: Stories of personal triumph from the frontiers of brain science.* Penguin Books.

Dyer, W. W. (2009). *You'll see it when you believe it: The way to your personal transformation.* William Morrow.

Fillmore, C. (2005). *The revealing word: A dictionary of metaphysical terms.* Unity House. (Original work published 1959)

Flavell, J. H. (1979). Metacognition and cognitive monitoring: A new area of cognitive-developmental inquiry. *American Psychologist, 34*(10), 906–911. https://doi.org/10.1037/0003-066X.34.10.906

Fox, E. (1934). *The sermon on the mount: The key to success in life.* HarperOne.

Friston, K. (2010). The free-energy principle: A unified brain theory. *Nature Reviews Neuroscience, 11*(2), 127–138. https://doi.org/10.1038/nrn2787

Goddard, N. (1944). *Feeling is the secret.* DeVorss & Company.

Goldsmith, J. (1947). *The Infinite Way.* DeVorss & Company.

Goleman, D. (2005). *Emotional intelligence.* Bantam Books.

Gray, J. H. (n.d.). *Emotional set point.* [Teaching reference; original source information not available.]

Hay, L. (1984). *You can heal your life.* Hay House.

Holmes, E. (1938). *The science of mind.* TarcherPerigee.

Jung, C. G., & Hull, R. F. C. (Trans.). (1973). *The collected works of C. G. Jung.* Routledge.

Kahneman, D. (2011). *Thinking, fast and slow.* Farrar, Straus and Giroux.

Lally, P., Van Jaarsveld, C. H. M., Potts, H. W. W., & Wardle, J. (2010). How are habits formed: Modelling habit formation in the real world. *European Journal of Social Psychology, 40*(6), 998–1009. https://doi.org/10.1002/ejsp.674

Leaf, C. (2013). *Switch on your brain: The key to peak happiness, thinking, and health.* Baker Books.

Levine, P. A. (2010). *Healing trauma: A pioneering program for restoring the wisdom of your body.* ReadHowYouWant.com.

Lieberman, M. D. (2000). Intuition: A social cognitive neuroscience approach. *Psychological Bulletin, 126*(1), 109–137. https://doi.org/10.1037/0033-2909.126.1.109

Lindsay, E. K., & Creswell, J. D. (2014). Helping the self-help others: Self-affirmation increases self-compassion and prosocial behaviors. *Frontiers in Psychology, 5,* 421. https://doi.org/10.3389/fpsyg.2014.00421

Lipton, B. H. (2005). *The biology of belief: Unleashing the power of consciousness, matter & miracles.* Hay House.

Maslow, A. H. (1943). A theory of human motivation. *Psychological Review, 50*(4), 370–396. https://doi.org/10.1037/h0054346

McCraty, R. (2004). Bioelectromagnetic communication within and between people. In P. J. Rosch & M. S. Markov (Eds.), *Bioelectromagnetic medicine* (pp. 541–562). Marcel Dekker.

Morter, S. (2020). *The energy codes.* Atria Books.

Myss, C. (1996). *Anatomy of the spirit.* Harmony.

Oschman, J. L. (2015). *Energy medicine: The scientific basis* (2nd ed.). Elsevier Health Sciences.

Pert, C. B. (1997). *Molecules of emotion: The science behind mind-body medicine.* Simon & Schuster.

Porges, S. W. (2011). *The polyvagal theory: Neurophysiological foundations of emotions, attachment, communication, and self-regulation.* W. W. Norton & Company.

Ruiz, D. M. (1997). *The four agreements.* Amber-Allen Publishing.

Schacter, D. L., Addis, D. R., & Buckner, R. L. (2007). Remembering the past to imagine the future: The prospective brain. *Nature Reviews Neuroscience, 8*(9), 657–661. https://doi.org/10.1038/nrn2213

Scovel Shinn, F. (1925). *The game of life and how to play it.* DeVorss & Company.

Siegel, D. J. (2012). *The developing mind: How relationships and the brain interact to shape who we are* (2nd ed.). The Guilford Press.

Van der Kolk, B. A. (2015). *The body keeps the score: Brain, mind, and body in the healing of trauma.* Penguin Books.

Veenman, M. V. J., Van Hout-Wolters, B. H. A. M., & Afflerbach, P. (2006). Metacognition and learning: Conceptual and methodological considerations. *Metacognition and Learning, 1*(1), 3–14. https://doi.org/10.1007/s11409-006-6893-0

Wood, W. (2019). *Good habits, bad habits: The science of making positive changes that stick.* Macmillan.

Recommended Books

Mind, Brain, and Behavior

- Barrett, L. F. (2020). *Seven and a half lessons about the brain.* Mariner Books.
- Doidge, N. (2007). *The brain that changes itself: Stories of personal triumph from the frontiers of brain science.* Penguin Books.
- Kahneman, D. (2011). *Thinking, fast and slow.* Farrar, Straus and Giroux.
- Wood, W. (2019). *Good habits, bad habits: The science of making positive changes that stick.* Macmillan.
- Siegel, D. J. (2012). *The developing mind: How relationships and the brain interact to shape who we are.* The Guilford Press.

Consciousness, Energy, and Healing

- Braden, G. (2021). *The wisdom codes: Ancient words to rewire our brains and heal our hearts.* Hay House.
- Damasio, A. R. (1999). *The feeling of what happens: Body and emotion in the making of consciousness.* Harcourt Brace.

- Lipton, B. H. (2005). *The biology of belief: Unleashing the power of consciousness, matter & miracles.* Hay House.
- Pert, C. B. (1997). *Molecules of emotion: The science behind mind-body medicine.* Simon & Schuster.
- Van der Kolk, B. A. (2015). *The body keeps the score: Brain, mind, and body in the healing of trauma.* Penguin Books.

Spiritual Growth and Metaphysical Wisdom

- Beckwith, M. B. (2011). *Life visioning: A transformative process for activating your unique gifts and highest potential.* Sounds True.
- Dispenza, J. (2012). *Breaking the habit of being yourself: How to lose your mind and create a new one.* Hay House.
- Fillmore, C. (1959/2005). *The revealing word: A dictionary of metaphysical terms.* Unity House.
- Holmes, E. (1938). *The science of mind.* TarcherPerigee.
- Myss, C. (1996). *Anatomy of the spirit.* Harmony.

Personal Transformation and Purpose

- Brown, B. (2020). *The gifts of imperfection.* Hazelden.
- Clear, J. (2018). *Atomic habits.* Avery.
- Dyer, W. W. (2009). *You'll see it when you believe it: The way to your personal transformation.* William Morrow.
- Morter, S. (2020). *The energy codes.* Atria Books.
- Ruiz, D. M. (1997). *The four agreements.* Amber-Allen Publishing.

Classic Metaphysical Texts and New Thought Pioneers

- Fox, E. (1934). *The sermon on the mount: The key to success in life.* HarperOne.
- Goddard, N. (1944). *Feeling is the secret.* DeVorss & Company.
- Goldsmith, J. (1947). *The Infinite Way.* DeVorss & Company.
- Scovel Shinn, F. (1925). *The game of life and how to play it.* DeVorss & Company.
- Hay, L. (1984). *You can heal your life.* Hay House.

These are some of the voices that walked beside me on my own journey of remembering. May they walk
beside you, too.

~DrSue

www.ingramcontent.com/pod-product-compliance
Lightning Source LLC
Chambersburg PA
CBHW042057150726
48005CB00032B/1145